Keeping Silent

A Childhood Lost

You are Special!

John 14:20

Estella Stone

Estella Stone

If I say, "The dark will screen me,
night will hide me in its curtains,"
yet darkness is not dark to thee,
the night is clear as daylight.

PSALM 139:11

When darkness overtakes her,
light will come bursting in.

PSALM 112:4

Contents

Foreword

This is the true account of my devastatingly painful childhood. I have several purposes in sharing the details of my horrific abuse. First and foremost, I want you to know that your identity does not have to be the one branded on you by others or yourself. Identities can be handed down, but they can also be revealed by a loving Heavenly Father. Who you are is not how you are treated but who God says you are. I want you to know that God smiles at you in wonder and delight regardless of your circumstances or what you may have done.

Secondly, I want you to be able to identify your own sufferings through my story. Hurt may come in many forms and in varying degrees, but it is still hurt and it still wounds the heart. It is only in recognizing that hurt and its cause that we can come to terms with it and the effect it has had on us.

Lastly, I want to share how I survived and persevered in the midst of crushing circumstances and unimaginable grief. I want you to know that there is always hope even in the darkest moments of life. I write my story with the expectation that you will be encouraged and see Jesus, Our Light, in the midst of your own despair. We may never understand why we encounter suffering or evil in this world, but we can rest knowing that Jesus will never leave us or forsake us regardless of who we are, our race, color, where we have come from, or performance in life. Wherever you may be on the trail of life, may you take heart through *Keeping Silent* in the God who always hears.

In Christ's abiding love,
Estella Stone
March 2017

Keeping Silent

1

Breaking Ground

I longed for freedom as I stood on the precipice that surrounded our lovely brick home, envying the strong wind that blew unrestrained through my long, dark, curly hair. I closed my eyes and thought of earlier days, before endless hours of being locked away, before surprise attacks, punishments, hunger pains, and stomach cramps. Beneath my feet was a tall, steep, brick retaining wall around three sides of our home. Our home was the first to be constructed on this particular part of the mountain. It wasn't really a mountain, more like a hill; but I always called it our "Mountain." The land before us and beside us was barren and undeveloped —not unlike my soul after years of crushing abuse. Our Mountain overlooked the entire town of Vulture Valley (pop. 30,000). Anyone could come along and erect a new development around us, if they chose, just as my parents could construct around me any life that they desired for me.

I was only a year old when my parents began to build our new and glorious home. It was large, by our standards, and in the shape of a square, with a courtyard in the middle. I was told that I had crawled through the wet concrete of that courtyard. Little did I know, at that age, that this event would portend the life that lay before me: trapped, crouching, and crawling on my hands and knees just to survive and obtain basic needs. Behind our new home, on the Mountain, was a dense stand of cedar trees. An old, large rock cistern was only a stone's throw from our backyard, but it was concealed by the overgrowth of sap-encrusted trees. I had come to love the brief moments when I escaped up the Mountain to get a bird's-eye view of our little town, and cherished the times I spent hiking and riding my bicycle with my brother in those wild spaces. The harsh world seemed so far away when we were lost in our play land. We spent many days building forts and swings and trying to avoid sticker plants and rattlesnakes. Those pleasant adventures did not last long, though. The day would come when I could only dream of hiking up our mountain—so close, yet so far away.

No one suspects the horrible things that go on in this beautiful house, I thought as I leapt off the wall onto the soft grass. A deep sigh stole my breath as I made my way back to the house. The sun was still up, but it had already begun to set inside me: it was Friday, Dad was away on a business day trip, and Mom was furious about something, but I couldn't figure out why.

My parents, Donna and Clark Stone, were very successful and, above all, very intelligent. You would need intelligence to conceal, so carefully, the dark secrets that entangled our lives. My father ran an oil and land brokerage while my mother spent most of her time at home. She had begun her college degree and would later finish it in Hotel, Restaurant, and Institutional Management; I often thought how ironic that was, given the constant hunger my brother and I suffered. My mind drifted to the days of my early childhood, straining to pull a single happy memory of my mother out of my mental filing cabinet. Back then, to make extra money, she had catered for big weddings; I had loved licking the icing and batter off the spoon after she was finished preparing the cake, and when asked in kindergarten what I wanted to be when I grew up, I replied, "A caterer like my mom, so that I can lick the spoon." At times she would also substitute-teach for the local school district. But all that was before she shut herself—and us—away.

Two years and one day after I was born, my brother came into this world. So then there were a little girl and a little boy living in that large house on the hill along with their parents. Both of us had blond hair, but my eyes were dark brown while my brother's were blue as the ocean.

Hearing my mom's angry voice coming from the kitchen, I walked with trepidation through the front door and past my shiny black piano. One day a man had come to our house and told my mom that he would sell her a piano for ten thousand dollars. It was a beautiful Yamaha, black with a lustrous polyurethane finish, and Mom always said, "God spoke to me that day and said, 'If you buy this piano, I will fill your house with music.'" Music had indeed come from my fingers, but all I heard right now were screams: Mom was furious about something. I could only try to imagine what could possibly have angered her now.

"How many times have I told you, Estella, that the forks have to be pointed *down* into the silverware basket? Look at that fork!" she screamed in my face. "It's pointed up. You disobedient child!"

I felt myself being thrust to the cold tile floor, and then she was on top of my stomach, straddling me. It was a good thing she only weighed ninety-five pounds. Then she grasped my curly-topped head between her bony hands and began to bang it against the floor. She slapped me across the face, first on one side and then on the other, and I closed my eyes, wincing in pain. That brought another slap; I wasn't supposed to wince. Suddenly she jumped off, picked me up, and slammed me up against the wall so that she faced me. Then she let go.

"I'm sorry, Mom, I didn't notice that fork turned around."

"That is not the answer I was looking for, young lady. Stop defending yourself!" This was followed by another slap. Why did I always have to defend myself? Why did I flinch? I always said and did the wrong thing. I would try harder next time. She dragged me into the carpeted living room and thrust me to the ground again, sat on me, and repeated what she had done before, but at least this time I was on carpet.

"Now get back into the kitchen!" she barked.

Trembling as she jerked me up again, I staggered back to the kitchen sink under her ever-present shadow. I still needed to finish loading the dishwasher. She had thrown all the dishes from the top rack back into the sink, so I started to reload them into the dishwasher. My hands shook as I grasped one of the plastic containers.

"The cups go in *this* way, on *this* side!" she shouted.

I reached for another of the dishes she had hurled back into the sink. The minutes seemed to crawl by as I felt her glare upon my red face, still stinging where her hot hand had struck my cheek. Embarrassment gripped me as I thought about Dad returning that evening. How would I face him? He would hear about this, my "disobedience" at the dishwasher; only God knew what would happen then.

My father was a kind man to all who knew him; in the case of my mother, a little too kind, in fact, as he would blindly do whatever she commanded. He was nothing more than her puppet half the time. However, I did find a certain comfort in knowing he was around, a comfort that my mom would later strip away completely, using careful tactics. For now, though, Mom's hand was stayed slightly when he was around. Dad would tuck my brother and me in at night after our Bible reading and, sometimes, a good story. He was such a good storyteller! We would sit outside together on the brick retaining wall, at sunset, and stare off over the small town of Vulture Valley while he told make-believe stories of far-off countries and a lion that was very powerful. It was only later that I discovered he was telling stories from C. S. Lewis's *Chronicles of Narnia.*

"Estella, where are you? Did you not hear what I just said? I said, Scrub the sink when you're done, and don't use the rough side of the sponge, or you'll scratch the sink!" Mom scolded. Without warning she gripped my arm again, digging her fingernails into my flesh, and flung me to the other side of the kitchen close to the microwave. "And you need to wipe out the microwave, too."

I lost myself in thought about one of my best friends, Lauren. Lauren's house was fun, although she often came to mine. One day when I was at Lauren's, and they were out of milk, she and her mom had walked into the kitchen where I sat eating my cereal.

"You didn't have any milk," I had explained to Lauren's mom, "so I just used grape soda. My mom doesn't allow me to have anything with sugar in it. This is delicious!" Lauren and her mother had laughed.

Sometimes, Lauren rode the bus home with me. I always enjoyed having her over and coming up with novel ideas to keep ourselves amused. One day we had decided to melt crayon shavings in a paper cup.

"We could use the microwave," I said.

"Yeah, that's a good idea," said Lauren. We stood with our noses pressed against the microwave door, watching the carousel turn around and around. The crayon shavings were definitely melting. But suddenly, they began to bubble up and over the paper cup. Then the paper cup began to disappear.

"Oh, my gosh!" I screamed, whipping the microwave door open.

"Wow," said Lauren, wide-eyed.

I tried pulling the misshapen cup off the carousel, and melted crayon dripped everywhere. Right then, my mom walked into the room, and Lauren and I looked up with wonder. *What will she do?* I thought to myself. I knew Lauren was thinking the same thing.

"Y'all made a big mess," said Mom. "Go along and I will clean it up. Go on now and wash your hands, and let me clean up the floor."

"Wow, Lauren," I breathed, relief flooding my eyes. "I'm glad you were here. Mom didn't even get mad!"

Now the stench of the wet sponge brought my mind back to the present as I stared at the microwave. I wished Lauren was here now to protect me.

"Estella, you need to clean the seal around the microwave door," Mom snapped, as another slap met my already burning cheeks. All her orders were punctuated by slaps, and she always seemed to be watching my every move. But at least she couldn't know what I was thinking; I had my thoughts to myself. She walked away to the other side of the kitchen, and my tense body relaxed as I let my mind go back in time. I could comfort myself by escaping into my own daydream land, remembering—or imagining—pleasant things. On this occasion, though, memories of Lauren were coloured by the bleakness of the present reality:

"Could Estella come over to play today after church?" Lauren's mother asked mine one day.

"No, Estella has to go home today and clean the house," answered my Mom.

Lauren moved a year later, but we remained best friends, and she still came for visits. She and I enjoyed her overnight stays, playing in my bedroom with games and dolls.

One day while Lauren was there, Mom put me into the master closet. Her master closet, as we called it, was very large, with enough room for me to do a cartwheel in it. Dad had his own closet, so Mom didn't have to share space with much of his stuff. There were racks for hanging clothes, and shelves for other things, and every once in a while Mom would let me look in the jewelry box she kept there; I especially loved the "black" pearls with their luminous dark blue colour.

I didn't mind being put away in her dark closet. In fact, I always felt safer from Mom when she put me in there and deadbolted the door. However, I had missed being with my friend, and wondered what Lauren would find to do around the house while I was locked away. Lauren had gone home that day and told her mom, "Today was awful. Estella got locked in the closet. It was terrible, Mom. Also, her brother was in the master bathroom crying. He had a big red welt on his leg and it was from a board."

I wish I was deadbolted in the closet right now, where Mom couldn't get to me so *quickly*, I mused, as I continued cleaning the microwave.

Soon Dad came home, and Mom delivered a withering report of my "disobedience." I was too overwhelmed with embarrassment to look up at my kind father.

"Estella, your mother works hard for you kids every day, slaving away in the kitchen. The least you can do is exactly what she tells you to do," he commented.

Slaving away? I thought to myself. Was my mom a slave? My mind went to the children of Israel in Egypt. They had been slaves. I was very familiar with the Old and New Testaments, and read my Bible every day, searching intently for its meaning for me. God had delivered the Israelites; maybe someday he would deliver me. I needed to not despair, because to despair was to not trust God, it was to lose your hope in God. I would always hope in him no matter what happened in my life. I had no clue just how far I would be stretched in this area in the many long years to come.

I nodded at my dad. Now that was done. I was lucky this time; I had received nothing worse than a rebuke. It was time for dinner, so I sat down to eat and started chatting away as I usually did. I was often the last to eat because I talked so much.

After dinner Gabriel and I cleared the table, and by then it was almost bedtime. I liked reading my Bible right before bed. I needed something special from the Lord tonight, and I was given it: my daily devotional was perfect for the day I had just endured. The verse was Psalm 17:8: "Keep me as the apple of Your eye; hide me in the shadow of Your wings." That would be my prayer tonight! God always had a special way of showing me how different he was from anyone else. He was the kind of shadow that I wanted to be under, the kind of shadow that would shield me from the heat of day.

2

School

In the third grade I began going to a new school, Magnet Elementary School. The principal, Mrs. Broughton, was friends with my Granny, my dad's mom, who lived in our home town. My teacher, Mrs. Cain, was very nice. My best friend Madison was in my home classroom, and she and I loved helping the boys who had dyslexia. We helped them at the teacher's request.

I was just beginning to notice that I felt different from other kids, and I wanted someone to pay attention to me. In reading class my desk was in the front, closest to the reading chart. I loved my reading teacher. *If only I could be loved by my reading teacher,* I thought longingly. *But she is just a teacher and can't take me home with her like a daughter.*

Soon after starting at that school, I attended a birthday party at the YMCA. The YMCA was where I took gymnastics, and during the summer I attended a day camp at the same facility. It was a very popular place to celebrate birthdays. When the party was over I stood outside, crying as I waited for Granny to pick me up. I was going to spend the night with her.

"Why are you crying?" said Granny.

"I didn't get to eat any cake," I replied, as the tears streamed down my face. Granny didn't say anything more; she knew I had followed Mom's orders: no sugar. Concern and heartbreak cut across her face, and the next morning she cheered me up by making me a cup of hot carob. It tasted almost like hot chocolate. Gran was the best!

My gymnastics class at the YMCA was offered through our school's extended day program and took place at the end of the school day. Afterwards I would arrive wearily at the bus stop just as the sun was setting. My mom would be at the bus stop to pick me up, and we would drive home to darkness. *I have homework to do, thank God,* I thought as we drove home one evening. *Maybe Mom will leave me alone if I stay busy.* And, mercifully, she did. I finished my homework and practiced the piano, and soon it was time for bed. But I was hungry.

"How could y'all be hungry after the wonderful meal your mother prepared?" Dad said. "She slaved away all day in the kitchen for you." I wondered if I was strange or different or just plain ungrateful. It had been a typical supper. I had eaten my little bit of apple—one slice—and then my portion of rice, one fourth of a cup. I was so hungry that night as I crawled into bed. Maybe I could eat from the other kids' lunches tomorrow. I would try to trade.

The next day I sat across from my schoolmates in the cafeteria.

"Would you like to trade with me?" I said to the person closest to me.

"What do you have?"

Worriedly, I glanced into my lunch pail. "I have cottage cheese. Could I trade you that for a fruit roll-up?"

"No way!"

"What about a little orange? I'll trade you a bag of chips for my half an orange."

It was no use. No one wanted to trade with me.

Day after day I ate my little bit of food, unseasoned and raw. *Just a little bit of butter or salt would make this spinach taste so much better*, I thought. We didn't keep butter in the house, though; butter was never allowed to touch my lips. But I was hungry, so butterless food would just have to be good enough.

3

Summer in Paradise

I had been packed off to Girl Scout camp for the first time years earlier; I was always the youngest in every class at school and in every camp group. My birthday fell at the end of August and my mom had placed me in school early. I learned to read when I was only three, because if I couldn't read the words pinned all over the house on index cards, I wasn't allowed to eat. Now I was nearing my ninth birthday and I was looking forward to escaping to Girl Scout camp for another two weeks out of the coming summer. I would miss... well, I wouldn't miss home, but I would miss something. I wasn't quite sure what. I knew I would feel lonely at camp, but I would drown it out with fun, the company of other kids, and Jesus: I loved reading my Bible and praying, and felt God's presence often when I was quiet and alone.

I also felt God's presence while I played the piano; I felt one with the music and put my whole body into it, and it seemed like a gift to me from God. I studied all the famous composers, but my heart was with Chopin. His music equaled the passion I felt in my heart. As long as I was alone at the piano I felt as if I was in another world, a world away from Mom's tyranny. Currently, Mom was my piano teacher. She had been teaching me since I was five, and slapping me through every lesson for every missed note. It seemed that I was about to surpass her in ability, though, which gave me hope that she would soon have to find me another teacher. In addition to classical composers, I also played beautiful hymn arrangements and was already in demand to play at churches and for weddings. Wherever I went, I was almost always able to find a piano, and even received donations from people when I played contemporary songs from TV shows and movies. My music library was always growing.

Finally, the day arrived when I was to go to camp. I was anticipating the food I would get to eat. I wouldn't be able to eat the sweet things other kids enjoyed, but maybe I would at least feel full at the end of each meal. Mom always gave careful instructions to camp staff regarding what I was allowed to eat. My tuck money was placed in an envelope, and each thing I bought was recorded on the outside of the envelope. I had found this out the hard way the previous year when I had purchased a candy bar: Mom had beaten me when I got home.

I waved goodbye to my dad, who was the one to take me to camp and drop me off. He had bought me ice cream on the way; I knew I must never tell Mom.

I was now standing in a large tent with many bunks. I shoved my trunk beneath my bed and rolled out my sleeping bag. Last year I had fallen out of the top bunk, so I was glad there were only regular beds in the tent this year. I met my new tentmates and my counselors; every summer I had high hopes of having a nice counselor. This year, one of my new friends from back home had come to camp at the same time as me, and it had been arranged that we would be in a tent together. I was so looking forward to sharing the fun of camp with her. I would hike and read and send letters to all my grandparents—and I would go swimming. Swimming was the best part of camp life. It was so hot in west Texas.

I looked around, wondering if maybe some of the girls I had met last year were here again.

"Candy!" I yelled excitedly when I saw my friend. "Candy, what's your favorite part of camp? I can't wait to go swimming! I wish there were horses here too—but oh, well. There is lots of other great stuff to do."

"We'll get to roast smores, Estella, and learn to build fires better than before." Right! I had forgotten about the smores. That was the best part about camp, even better than swimming! Earlier in the summer, Candy and I had helped to build fires at the Girl Scout day camp back home. I took great pride in my ability to build a good log cabin fire or teepee fire.

Soon it was time to go to the great mess hall where we would eat our dinner. Candy and I walked together.

"Wow. Would you look at that," I said in awe. "The 'gum tree' has even more gum stuck on it than it had last year. Look, Candy, look at all the different colors of bubble gum." We stared at the rainbow of bumps and blobs.

"Well, I'll add to it later when I'm done chewing this piece," she said as she stretched a large chunk of slimy purple stuff from between her teeth. I stared up at the great tree. Was that an oak? Its trunk was massive and almost covered in chewed bubble gum. It looked like a million rainbows swirled into one.

Later that night we lay on our cots. "Candy, are you still awake?"

"Yes. Do you hear that noise?"

"It's the mice scurrying on the tent flaps."

"I know. I can hear them." The mice seemed in such a hurry to go nowhere. Where would they all go except to the other side of the tent? Up and down they ran, up one side of the tent roof, over my head, and down the other side, over Candy's head. Later on in years to come I would look back on this night and think of how my life reminded me of the mice in their futile running back and forth. But now I drifted off to sleep. Tomorrow would be a fun day.

I awoke to the sound of camp counselors calling to girls. Candy and I jumped hurriedly into our clothes, and a few minutes later were trapezing across the gigantic swing bridge with the rest. We crossed one after the other, counting to ten before starting out behind our buddy: we had a buddy system to help keep us safe. Soon we were all back at the gum tree, gathered for instructions.

"Okay, girls. Listen up. Today you get to hunt for your breakfast. All over the yard are hidden boxes of cereal. Go and find whatever kind of cereal you'd like to eat."

I would hunt for Fruit Loops. I had first tasted Fruit Loops at a friend's house, and I loved them. I would never tell my mom, of course. It had to be the most wonderful breakfast I would ever have at camp.

"On your mark! Get set! Go!" yelled the camp counselor. Off I scurried, running from tree to tree, searching for my favorite cereal like it was treasure, and then sitting down with the others to enjoy it. What a delicious outdoor breakfast!

Later Candy and I were sitting around the center of our own campsite with all the other girls in our section, when suddenly I jumped up screaming, tearing at my shirt.

"Someone! Quick, help me get Estella's shirt off!" cried one of my friends.

"Owwww," I moaned. What could it be? In seconds they had my shirt ripped off.

"It's a good thing this is an all girl's camp," said one of my friends. Crawling up my bare arm was a spider that had apparently been biting me. I used to like watching spiders. Not anymore!

After I'd donned a new shirt, my buddy and I walked to the nurse's office. Every day after that I would have to get treated for my spider bites. How could one spider have so many teeth? I probably had ten to fifteen bites! Ughhh. Everyone was so nice to me, though, and it didn't seem to hurt so much after the nurse put on the special cream. Besides, that night we would get to roast smores—my favorite thing! Who cared about spider bites when smores were around the corner?

Before long my time at camp was over, and I was picked up by my Great-Granddad Eric. I would go to stay with my other great-grandparents for a little while before getting passed off to Granddad, Gran, and my Aunt Jade along with my brother. That would be my favorite part of the whole summer.

"Six Flags, here we come! Wet'n'Wild, here we come!" I said to my brother. "Aunt Jade's famous nachos, instant peaches-and-cream oatmeal, and as much food as I can eat, here we come! I can't wait!" Granddad and Gran lived in Dallas, Texas, not far from where my Aunt Jade lived. As soon as Gabriel and I arrived, Gran took us to the store and bought junk food. She fed us sandwiches for lunch, something I never got to eat at home. One of my favorite things to do at Gran's was stand and stare into her great big pantry. One day I opened the door to see what snack I might choose for myself, and lo and behold, there was Gran, looking silly, standing in the pantry with a can of cheese spray in one hand and a cracker in the other. Gabriel and I had gotten her completely hooked on that simple snack.

Gran always took us shopping for toys, too. I had started to collect Cabbage Patch dolls and all the little clothes and things that go with them; I loved their chubby little faces and their soft cloth bodies. Gran and Granddad let our friends come over to play in their great big backyard full of bushes, tall climbing trees, flowers, and stone steps. We made a game for ourselves: start at one end of the semi-circle of dense bushes and try to get to the other end without touching the ground. That was so much fun.

And I loved climbing. One day I shimmied up the largest tree in the very center of the backyard, a tree whose trunk was many feet in circumference and could be clearly seen from the kitchen window. I could find no place to sit up there, though, so once I had reached the big branches far above the ground, I quickly climbed back down. Exploring around the great backyard, I soon found a piece of wire netting that piqued my curiosity. It was very strong, and reminded me of a hammock. *This is perfect*, I thought. *Now, how to attach it to the branches?* I rummaged in my grandfather's shed, where I came upon several very long nails. They looked like railroad spikes, just like I'd seen on "Little House on the Prairie," one of my favorite TV shows. I took the nails and hurried back up the tree with the wire netting, carefully nailing it to the most suitable limbs. I had just begun to relax in my new hammock when I heard my grandfather calling to me from below.

"Estella! Oh, Stelllllla! Have you seen my piece to the roof?"

"No, Granddad, I haven't seen it," I called down, and relaxed again. Ahhhh, what a *perfect* summer day!

"Are you sure you haven't seen my piece of the roof, Estella? It was lying right here." He pointed to the ground.

Oh, no! I gulped. I quickly pointed to where I was sitting. "Here it is, Granddad."

But he wasn't mad at all. He went to fetch a ladder, and although it took him half the day, he removed each railroad spike, as I called them. Then he nailed boards up between the branches so I could have a place to sit. I tried out my new perch. It was the perfect retreat from the world below.

That night my brother and I sat curled up in front of Gran's bedroom television. We each had a bowl of ice cream, awash in a sea of chocolate syrup; I couldn't believe Gran would let us into her bedroom with such a messy dessert. This was the life!

Too bad it had to end. Soon summer was over, and my brother and I returned home. I missed my summer days at Gran and Granddad's house; the memory made life at home seem especially uncomfortable. Mom wasn't happy, that much was obvious, and I didn't know what to do. Every second that I could, I escaped into my books. Mom had always stressed the importance of reading, and I knew it was advantageous for me to read from the wealth of literature our family had collected over the years. Besides, I loved reading. I could escape my present circumstances, at any moment, by entering someone else's world—*if* I wasn't engaged with a myriad of chores. Mom and Dad used to comment, "If a tornado hit while you were reading, the whole world would fall apart and you would never know it." I had to agree. I gazed at the trophy I'd recently won at school for reading the most books; I had received it as a third grader in competition with kids in fourth and fifth grade, so I was greatly honored. My mom had been proud of me that day.

Mrs. Cain had been a wonderful third grade teacher. She seemed slightly gruff at times, but I had enjoyed her class and she had helped fan the flames of reading that my mother had already lit. Of course, the accident with my big toe had helped spur me on to more reading. I had stubbed my toe earlier that year, so badly that it had required surgery. While it was healing I had been ordered to go to the lunchroom early each day, wearing my special bootie to ensure the safety of my bandaged foot. Being alone in the lunchroom wasn't much fun, but I knew that the quiet had been good for me, and it had given me precious extra minutes for reading.

Now third grade had passed and fourth grade lay before me. *I wonder what my new teacher will be like this year?* I thought. My ninth birthday was approaching, with my brother's birthday the day after. Mom had always thrown us great parties when we were younger, but now that I was older Mom found it challenging to figure out what to feed kids when sugar was absolutely off the table. I always felt like our real celebrating was done in Dallas at my grandparents' house.

4

Things Get Worse

I was pushing the soft, navy blue cushioned chairs under the round glass table that I had just polished so carefully with Windex. I always made sure there was not a single finger smudge on the glass top.

"Estella, make sure the chairs are perfectly in place," said Mom.

I always checked to see that the chairs were in precisely the right position beneath the glass tabletop. Every time we walked past the chairs and bumped them with our hips by mistake, I had to make sure they were arranged correctly again in their designated spots.

As I examined the table for smudges, my mind flashed back to when I was only four. I had climbed up on the glass table in order to push harder on my Play-Doh Fun Maker, having unknowingly put so much Play-Doh into the special compartment that none could come out. I had climbed up on my knees and leaned in until the plastic lever snapped. Forward I went, sailing straight into the large, opulent glass bowl full of glass marbles and silk flowers that graced our kitchen table as a centerpiece. My head had careened straight through the bowl, and I could still remember standing up and staring down at my blood-soaked dress. It was a dark blue dress with flowers on it; I never saw it again.

As usual, my parents had not taken me to the doctor, preferring to treat me themselves. They had placed little butterfly bandages on my nose and head, and I remembered thinking how cute they were. *I didn't cry that time,* I thought to myself. *I don't cry when stuff hurts; I only cry when I'm disappointed and lonely.* I tried eyeballing my own nose, remembering, and my eyes crossed. The scar still spread across my nose in a line that tapered from thick at one end to thinner at the other. I touched the little indelible crater that remained on my forehead. *I probably should've had stitches,* I thought. But Mom did not like taking us to the doctor. Only in extreme emergency, or if we needed a note for camp, were we ever taken to the doctor. *No one likes sitting in a doctor's office,* I thought.

Suddenly I whirled around. Mom was screaming.

"I want to kill myself! I just want to kill myself!" she shrieked, slamming her head against the kitchen wall. "I can't stand it here!" She threw her body against the door frame of the small side room adjacent to the kitchen, and then began wildly pounding her head against the clean white wall. Slowly, her fingers lifted above her head, curled, and then slowly scratched her soft, pale skin all the way down her face. Her fingernails dug into each arm, and she began to claw savagely at herself. She screamed again, and strange stuff dribbled out of her mouth.

"Mom," I whispered frantically, "you're hurting yourself. Please stop, Mom!" I wrapped my arms around her, but she swung at me and I lost my balance, toppling back toward the counter that housed the kitchen sink. My hands hit the cold, hard tile as I tried to break my fall. Scrambling to my feet, I backed away quickly in an effort to avoid any more harmful encounters. Dad came rushing into the room.

"Donna! Donna!" he kept repeating, and then, to no one in particular, or to me, "She's having another of her attacks."

Somehow we felt like we were to blame, my brother and I. Was that a glare my dad had just shot our way? It pierced my heart. It hurt to see Mom this way, and to think that we were supposed to be the cause. But tomorrow was a new day; maybe tomorrow Mom would be better.

Tomorrow came, and Mom was worse than ever. She didn't get better after that. She slapped me routinely—not once in a while, but all the time, repeatedly; once she started, she just kept on going. She was worst when she stopped taking her meds. She was on anti-depressants, but now and then she would decide she was better and no longer needed them.

"I'm doing great now," she'd say. "I don't need this anymore." And she'd stop them cold. Whenever she did this, Gabriel and I knew we could expect a reign of terror.

In the kitchen, which was the hub of our life, Mom was always trying to teach me things: how to prepare a dish of beans, wash vegetables, and keep everything clean. But all her instructions and all my tasks were punctuated by slaps. It got so that if she raised her arm, I would flinch automatically. I just couldn't help flinching if Mom came close.

"Stop flinching!" she yelled once in a frenzy. "I wasn't going to hit you!" And a slap seared across my face. I let the sponge drop down into the sink.

"Estella, see that water spot on the faucet? Why is there a water spot on the faucet? You are supposed to buff it with the Windex cloth."

"I wasn't to that part yet," I explained. But explanation was futile. She flung my helpless body against the wall close by. As she raised her hands I turned to shield myself, and felt her fingernails dig into my back and down my arms.

Oh no, I thought, my heart sinking, *Now I won't be able to go out. I won't be allowed to go anywhere until it's healed.* She dropped to her knees, her head below mine, and clawed at the back of my legs. Then, like a lioness with her prey, she dragged me through the house. *Oh no,* I thought again, guessing what was coming. All at once she flung me down, into the hallway between our bedrooms, raced to Dad's closet, and jerked it open with such rage that the house shook; I heard the slam as the steel doorknob collided with the wall, and the clang of hangers as everything on the inside of the closet door swung wildly. Mom was getting the belt. She ran back to me with it and thrashed me, blow upon blow. I felt helpless and ashamed. I wanted to scream, but I was never able to make a sound: someone might hear, and above all, no one must ever hear.

The sun rose, and with it, hope in my heart. I skipped through the house. It was a new day, a school day! A chance to get away from home. Mom checked me roughly from top to bottom; I stood naked before her as she scrutinized every mark on my body.

"You must make sure the scratches stay covered up," she barked.

I looked down. The belt marks were almost gone.

"Come on, finish your morning chores, and then come eat your oatmeal," she commanded.

Not the oatmeal! I knew I had to eat it, because if I didn't I'd be an ungrateful wretch, and besides, she slaved away during the early morning hours to make the special oatmeal; it was "extra healthy," she said. I climbed up on the bar stool and stared into my bowl of trepidation. I liked the instant oatmeal that Aunt Jade served us, but this greyish glop tasted awful: no sugar, no salt, no butter, only a few drops of nonfat milk.

I gulped it down, knowing what awaited me, and sure enough, it wasn't long before I felt agonies of stomachache, as I always did after eating Mom's oatmeal. I was doubled over with spasms of pain. I knew it was dangerous to be sick with Mom; how could I be sick with her here? In a few days she would be gone; she was taking my little brother with her to another town two hours away, where she would go back to school to work on her degree. Yippee! But for now I had to endure. I lay curled up in the black wing chair, clutching my stomach as another cramp seized me. How could a little bit of oatmeal cause so much suffering? I noticed the pink embroidered flowers in the black fabric of the chair. *I wish I could disappear into this chair like one of those flowers and never return,* I moaned inaudibly. I knew that Mom was aware how much the oatmeal always upset my stomach. Why was she torturing me on purpose? A few minutes later she came from the kitchen sink and stood over me, mocking me as I writhed in pain.

"You are such a disobedient child, such a disobedient child, and you will just have to go to school late today." Finally, she left me alone.

Later that morning I had recovered enough to leave for

After I left home, I discovered that my mother had doctored my oatmeal for three years with the intent of poisoning me.

school. I was weak and worn out from all the cramping, and I felt alone at school, but I was so happy to be away from home, and smiled and laughed as I did my schoolwork. I was looking forward to when Mom would leave, and it would be just me and Dad until Christmastime. Yay! Mom was going away to college and taking Gabriel with her. They would live in another town, Lubbock, and Dad and I would stay at home.

Once Mom and Gabriel had gone, I was allowed to wake up on my own and pick out my own clothes every morning. Mom always put me in clothes that were too small. Now, finally, I could choose clothes that fit! And in the evenings, Dad and I would eat ice cream; I knew this was to be our secret. In the afternoons, when Dad was still at work, I was sometimes sent to Granny and Grampy's house. I loved being there. Granny always bought honey and carob just for me, and would gently tickle my back at night with her fingernails in a way that felt good. She was scratching my back, but it was not the kind of scratching Mom did; it was comforting and relaxing. I would get to spend the night with Granny and Grampy. I was glad they lived in our own town; my other grandparents lived five hours away, and I only saw them a couple of times a year.

One weekend when Dad had to work, I ended up in Lubbock with my mom and brother. Sometimes Mom came home on the weekends, and sometimes we went up there. I didn't know where Dad's work had taken him, but he was not around. Mom had somewhere important to go, to talk with an important man.

"When I return, let me in," she said as she left.

I remembered the long, agonizing hours of waiting for her terrifying return on this and similar nights. I knew that any moment I would hear her pounding on the door. I sat motionless in the dark room, waiting. It was so peaceful with Mom away; even a few hours or just a few minutes was a relief, and I didn't want her to come back. The moment of return would always come, though, when she would knock on the door, and I would have to let her back in, and peace would be shattered. When would the knock come? Why did she have to return? She always came back.

I sat in the seat across from the little trailer door, waiting. At last I nodded off to sleep—and then, bang, bang, bang. I opened the door, and Mom stormed into the trailer that was her temporary home in Lubbock. She hit me across the face over and over again, turned toward my little brother, and slapped him too. Then she came back for me. I didn't know why she was angry; she didn't need a reason.

"Why did you have to be born?" She picked up my crouching body and flung me across the room so that I crashed into some chairs. Huddled in the corner of the room, I wished to God that I had never been born. God, why did you let me be born? Why? Why? *I want to be with you right now, Jesus. Take me to where you are.*

It was dark outside; I wanted to hide in the darkness. I brought my knees to my chest and wrapped my arms around them. I felt safe in the dark, but Mom could always see me. I was fooling myself to think I could hide, but for just a moment or two I felt safe surrounded by blackness. Maybe her anger would subside soon. Maybe she would forget I was here if I stayed huddled in the dark corner. How I hated that trailer home! I wondered how my brother fared there, all alone with Mom.

But she loved him so much more than she loved me. Perhaps it was not all bad for him.

5

It's a Hard Knock Life

We were all back at home now in our own big kitchen in Vulture Valley; the fall semester was over, and Mom and Gabriel had moved back home. I was standing in the middle of the tile floor, and Mom was standing before the double ovens just across from our refrigerators, giving angry directives as usual.

"You must never, never, *never* open the fridge unless you absolutely have to, or the seal will break," she said, "and we must see to it that the seal on the fridge never goes. You must pile the food on the counter next to the fridge, and then, all at once, you had better put everything away in the fridge very quickly, so as not to let the cold air out." Then, "You are so very pretty," she sneered at me. Was my own mother jealous of my looks? "Everyone around here says that you look exactly like Julia Roberts. There was a special documentary on Julia Roberts, and everyone who saw it said that you look just like her when she was young." She started inching toward me.

"You are just like your Granny: always smiling and talking, and everyone loves you." She began to raise her voice. "Everyone loves you!" She made no attempt to hide her jealousy. "I hate you," she blurted out. "I hate you!"

I know, I thought. *More oatmeal coming right up.*

Later that week I was given a Dum-Dum sucker by my teacher at school. I peeled back the colored paper. *Mom will never know,* I thought, *since I always ride the bus home.* I took one lick of the sweet treat and my whole mouth rejoiced! I hadn't had sugar in a very long time. It was exquisite, and I was still hungry from the meager lunch I'd been sent to school with; actually, I was always hungry. As I licked the sucker a second time, I felt a clobber on my back.

"Estella, what are you doing?" yelled my mom. "You know better than to eat stuff like that!" She took me to the car and began hitting and slapping me repeatedly.

"But Mom," I pleaded, "I haven't eaten much of it at all."

"Estella, don't lie to me. Look how small the sucker is. Do you expect me to believe you've only had a few licks?"

"Mom, I barely had any of the sucker before you got here."

She had surprised me with her visit. Why of all days did she have to pick today to come to the school? She glanced around, then marched off back into the school. A few minutes later she returned.

"Apparently you're right. It did start out as a very small sucker," she conceded, without remorse. What did it matter now? She had already hit me too many times to count, and now she was going to be perfectly content just because she'd found out the sucker was small. I just did not understand my mother.

The days drudged past, but I took pleasure in my time at school. At home I occupied every spare minute reading books and playing with my rabbits. One of them, who was very large, nevertheless managed to get into places where I couldn't find her. I was looking for her one day and stooped down in the garage to peer under Mom's car. There was Thumper, under the car again!

"Come on. Come on," I coaxed. "I don't want you eaten by Mom's car!" But it was no use: Thumper would not come out. I snatched up a bowl filled with cat food. "This is why you weigh thirty-six pounds," I told her. "You're always eating the cat food, you rascal!" As soon as I waved the cat food in front of Thumper, out from under the car she bounded. I traipsed back into the house, and decided to read one of my favorite mystery novels, a Nancy Drew. I also liked Trixie Belden, the Hardy Boys, the Bobbsey Twins, and best of all, good old-fashioned classics. After reading, I would practice the piano again: with choir and bell choir at school, dancing, and piano, my life—apart from the repeated confrontations with my mother—was saturated with song. It was how I kept my balance amid all the upheaval at home.

The year was passing quickly, and I was looking forward to a special trip with my great-grandparents, who lived a couple of hours away: they would be taking me out of town to see the musical *Annie*. I loved the songs from *Annie*, especially "It's a Hard Knock Life." Mom had an old record of the musical, and I would play it and sing along at the top of my lungs while I dusted the furniture and did other housework. It helped to make the many hours of drudgery pass more quickly. Now the day of leaving town was drawing nearer and nearer, and I was in my homeroom at school, trying in vain to pay attention. But we were studying stuff I had already memorized; I was bored with it and could not focus with such a wonderful prospect looming on the horizon. *I can't wait!* I thought. Holding up my science book for cover, I sneaked my Nancy Drew book in front and became engrossed in the mystery; I didn't even notice my teacher standing next to me and peering over my shoulder, and before I knew it I was temporarily grounded from reading. That was a bitter punishment for the likes of me!

One day shortly after that, when I arrived at school, I began to feel cramping stabs of pain in my belly. *That's funny,* I thought, *I didn't eat any oatmeal today. Besides, the pain of the oatmeal always hits well before I can even get to school.*

"My stomach hurts," I informed my teacher.

"Well, then, I'd better get the office to call your mom," she said.

"Oh no! Please don't call my mom. I'm all right. Really, I will be fine. See? I'm better now. Just please, don't call my mom. I'll just stay here."

I went to my next class: Music. I had a different teacher for this class. My stomach began to cramp again, so I went up to my Music teacher and told her I was in pain. Like my other teacher, she offered to call my mom, and again I resisted. Few things could be worse than having Mom come and fetch me from school.

But the same thing happened in Library class later in the day. The cramps were getting worse and worse, and I couldn't help myself: I mentioned to my Library teacher how bad I was feeling. Again came the perfectly sensible reply, "I'll give your mom a call," and again I spoke a resounding "No!" I knew they all thought I was lying, but little did they know how scared I was to go home, especially sick. You just weren't sick around Mom. I didn't care what they thought, I simply could not allow myself to go home sick!

Finally school let out and I climbed onto the bus, off to my gymnastics program. By the time I got into the YMCA building I couldn't move, so I just sat on the sidelines and watched. Afterward, I managed to make it home and just barely got into bed; Mom didn't even notice that I wasn't feeling well. *Thank you, God.* I was safe for one more day. I lay in bed thinking about God and about Jesus, my friend. Reaching for my Bible, I turned to a passage and began to read. It was Psalm 41:3: "The Lord will strengthen him on his bed of illness; You will sustain him on his sickbed." I read the same Scripture in another translation to get a clearer sense of the meaning. "He nurses him on his sickbed," the New English Version read.

"So, God, you are a nurse, too!" I whispered. After that everything became a blur. The night went on relentlessly, and so did my pain. I began vomiting uncontrollably, and knew I must be suffering from a bad case of the flu—the worst flu I'd ever had. I felt hot and achy all over. Sweat beaded on my forehead, but I was torn back and forth between freezing to death and burning up. Finally, the vomiting eased up and I fell asleep.

I awoke to Mom trying to pry me out of bed. It was already late morning: I had obviously missed school. I wanted to ask what was happening, but I felt too weak to speak, and sicker than I'd ever been in my life—so sick I didn't care about hiding it any more. I didn't even care what Mom did to me. Sometimes she was nice when I was sick, and sometimes she wasn't; I would just have to make that gamble. I could barely move, but Mom was pulling me out of bed; I didn't understand why I had to get out of bed when I was so sick. I fell halfway to the floor and then regained my footing. Mom grabbed my arm and began to half walk, half drag me toward her master bathroom. As I hobbled down the hallway, my right side suddenly gave way, and I started to go down. Mom had hold of my arm as I collapsed onto the carpet. Searing pain pierced my side and shot through my abdomen.

"Why did you do that, Estella?" Mom asked, in a tone that seemed slightly hostile, as if I were deliberately being difficult. All I could do was clutch my side, unable to respond, and at last she began to take in the seriousness of my condition. "Is that where it hurts, Estella?" she asked, and then, "Oh, my gosh," she gasped, frantically now; "Oh, my gosh!" She continued to help me down the long hallway. I was in a daze and couldn't understand why she was taking me to her bathroom. Finally, after what felt like the longest walk of my life, I arrived where Mom apparently wished me to be, and collapsed onto the carpet on my back. The pain intensified with each passing moment. Mom raced off to grab the great big gold medical book and flipped through the pages as she knelt by my side on the floor.

"Is this where it hurts?" She pushed on my stomach, and I winced in pain. "Oh, my gosh!" she said again, and half-carried me to the car as fast as she could manage, thrust me into it, and drove me to the hospital. Strangely, I began to feel slightly better—until the doctor, saying, "This might hurt," pressed briefly on my abdomen. Oh, it did hurt so badly!

I'll never forget the wonderful feeling of saying goodbye to that pain. A nurse came and gave me a shot to make me feel better, and it worked; the pain was suddenly gone! A few minutes later I was in the surgical theater. I now knew it was appendicitis and they would be taking out my appendix. The surgeon who attended me was very considerate; walking in and finding me semi-exposed in the hospital gown, he said immediately to the nurses, "Cover the girl up; by all means, cover the poor girl up."

"Estella, would you like a shot in the arm to put you to sleep, or would you like the mask?" he asked. I remembered Mom telling me that the mask makes you feel like you are suffocating, and since shots didn't bother me a bit, I confidently stuck out my arm.

"In the arm, please."

"Well, then," he said, a little surprised, "we'll just put some cream on your arm first to numb it up before the shot." I was quickly put to sleep. When I woke up from surgery, the first thing I asked was, "Where is my appendix?"

"We threw it away, Estella."

"Threw it away?! Well, can you get it back out of the trash? I want to see it."

"No, Estella, we can't get it out of the trash. It was too infected. It was oozing pus everywhere. There's no way we could keep that around."

"Oh," I said, disappointed. I just couldn't believe they hadn't saved it for me. Didn't they know I would want to see anything that was removed from my own body?

"Estella," said a nurse, "your pastor is here. He's outside those doors praying for you. Your parents are out there too." I couldn't believe the pastor had come all the way to the hospital just to pray for me. I was going to ask to see him, when all of a sudden I began to feel sick and weak; all my energy had been spent trying to get a look at my appendix. My eyes felt heavy, and I dropped off to sleep.

When I woke up again, it was with a feeling of deep disappointment as the realization came crashing down that I would not be going to visit my great-grandparents and see the musical *Annie*. I'd taken a trip to the hospital instead! But there they were, my great-grandparents, standing by my bed and watching me attentively as I emerged from my groggy sleep.

I smiled at the sight of them. Their presence was comforting, and I felt safe.

"Am I still going to be able to go see *Annie*?"

"No, darling. You are very, very sick. We are lucky to have you alive."

"What?! No *Annie*?! But I've waited so long to see it! Is there a chance we could go to a later showing?" I asked timidly.

"Honey, you are too sick, and need to rest," replied my grandmother. "You will be in bed for several weeks."

I groaned audibly at the thought of "resting" at home. Not only would I miss *Annie*, but I would miss school as well, and who knew what frame of mind Mom would be in; my time at home might be anything but restful. I took some comfort in the thought that she knew I had almost died. *Maybe Mom will be kind this time*, I thought. I turned my head to see her sitting in the corner of the hospital room.

I closed my eyes and pretended to be asleep, but in reality I was making my escape into the remembered sound of all the *Annie* songs I had listened to during the long and merciless hours of cleaning at home. Again I thought how listening to music while I cleaned made the time go by so much more quickly, and singing along brought so much comfort to my heart. *God must be in music!* I thought. *It's like C. S. Lewis said: "Music is the bridge to heaven."* In my mind I was singing "It's a Hard Knock Life" over and over again. *I wish I had died,* I told Jesus in my mind, and thought of Annie tenderly comforting the little scared girl at the beginning of the musical. I wanted someone to comfort me like that.

Music and reading were my chief refuge. *That's where I hide,* I said to myself. I thought of how hard Annie had to work, and how hard I had to work every minute I was at home, especially on weekends. Now I could hardly move; I would not be doing any cleaning for quite some time. Mom did not allow me to listen to music unless I was cleaning, so my refuge would be the many classic novels in our library at home. I would be doing all the reading I could. Disappointed as I was over the cancellation of my trip to see *Annie*, I smiled at the thought of no chores: Mom couldn't ask me to clean if I couldn't even walk! I finally drifted off to sleep accepting this new bittersweet reality.

Many people came to visit me each day at the hospital. Some would walk into my room and rush out; I knew it was because they were about to cry. Everyone said I looked very pale and far too thin, and their startled reactions made me understand just how sick I was. Even the teachers from my school put together a giant card and had many people sign it. My teachers said they were sorry for not taking me seriously when I'd told them I wasn't feeling well, not realizing how glad I was that they hadn't sent me home! But I couldn't explain that to them.

Now I could not go to school for quite a while; I would have to stay home. I was devastated, but continued to hope that since I had almost died, perhaps Mom would be nicer to me from now on, especially given how different she'd been since my admission to the hospital. One of the things I worried about was whether I'd ever again be strong enough to run track; I couldn't imagine walking right now, let alone running, but a kind nurse kept telling me that one day soon I would be back to normal and run so fast! It was as if God Himself was speaking the words, giving me hope. I *would* run again someday! I was given shots around the clock, and slept a lot; one night I dreamed that a gigantic tarantula was walking across all the balloons that filled my hospital room, and woke up terrified. My nurse came in to give me a bed bath.

"You can take a bath in bed?" I asked, surprised.

"You sure can." She explained the entire process to me.

Grampy brought me milkshakes every day. I felt so lucky! Mom had never allowed that kind of thing, and now seemed totally okay with it. I lived on milkshakes for a long time. I was laid up for about three weeks, and Mom was nice to me the entire time I was at home. Surely this boded well for a permanent change.

One day after I had come home, I walked into a room to find a new girl there, introduced to me as Lynda. She was a teenager, but seemed much older because of all the responsibilities she carried. She was there to help Mom around the house, watch my brother and me occasionally, help teach me school, and also work in my dad's office. Dad's office was in the game room for now.

"This is Estella," my mom said to Lynda. "We almost lost her. She was very sick when her appendix burst. Can you believe she hid the sickness from us? Can you believe she did that? She almost died, and it was all her own fault."

I smiled grimly at Lynda. She looked beautiful. I couldn't wait to get to know her.

Mom soon forgot that she had almost lost her only daughter. As soon as I was really well, she began to slip back into her old ways.

"I have to hide the food from the kids," I heard her explain one day to Lynda, whose job included straightening up the kitchen. "They would eat it if I left it out where they could find it." Food was hidden all over the kitchen.

Inevitably, oatmeal reappeared on the menu. I groaned. Would this never end? I forced myself to eat it, choking down every bite, knowing I would have just a few minutes before the stomach cramps would start. This would be the only food I would receive until lunch—if I could eat lunch,

that is. Lynda watched as Mom stood over me, mocking my hesitation as if it were mere rebellious pretense.

"These horrible, horrible children! I can't believe I gave birth to these horrible children. I can't believe they came out of my body! Estella is *such* a disobedient child, such a disobedient child."

I was late to school again. Things hadn't changed a bit: Mom still hated me. It seemed as if she hated Dad, too. I looked exactly like my father. Did I remind her too much of him?

"I can't believe I married a nobody from Vulture Valley," she barked at my dad. "I wanted to travel. I can't believe I married you." I was standing right there, but they didn't seem to care that I could hear every word. My heart bled for my father. He wasn't a nobody, not to me or my brother.

Meanwhile my little brother was having difficulty reading. I never dreamed what an important role this would play in my life. Mom decided she needed a special new phonics program, and someone was bringing it to the house to explain how it worked. Her name was Ann, and she had moved back to Vulture Valley after going to live somewhere else; her father-in-law and husband ran the chiropractic office were Mom always went. Ann pulled up to our house, got out of her car, and started up the long, inclined concrete walkway that ran through our front yard, eventually meeting several steps that formed a break between the retaining walls that surrounded our house. The instant I saw her, I knew that she was kindness walking. She smiled when she saw me, and gave me a hug. *Wow.* It had been so long since anyone had shown me that kind of affection, back on my trip to stay with my grandparents in Dallas. That seemed so long ago now.

Our neighbors down the street, friends of our family who gave me their daughter's clothes every year, began to strongly encourage my mom to let me go to First Baptist Church on Wednesday evenings. I was ecstatic. Ann attended First Baptist Church; I would get to visit with her often. Also, I would get to be in another bell choir besides the one at school. I would get to take a special class in music, drama, and choir as well as eat dinner at the church on Wednesday nights. I loved going to church! All my friends were there. It was often hard trying to relate to other kids when I felt so very alone, painfully aware that no one knew what my life was really like; but I was so happy to be gone from the house and around other people!

The best part about Wednesday night church was Ann. Every Wednesday night, she taught the preschool choir. She didn't stay for dinner, but I always arrived at church before her class of small children let out. One night I arrived just in time, and hovered around the door of Ann's choir classroom, waiting anxiously for her to emerge. I so looked forward to this. Ann was a mystery to me: I looked into her big green eyes and wondered how she could love me when I was such a terrible child.

The door squeaked open and lots of little children poured out of the room.

"Hi, Estella. How are you, Precious?" Ann gave me a tight hug. Just for that moment the whole world seemed a much happier place, and my face lit up in a broad smile. Life was good! We visited for a minute or two, and then Ann had to leave. My heart sank as I watched her walk away; I had waited all week for this, and now it was over in just a few minutes. But my heart leapt at the thought of dinner time, when I would at least be able to fill my empty stomach! Besides, I would see Ann at church again on Sunday, before and after the service. I always went to the adult choir room to find her on Sundays, and she always seemed so happy to see me. I had a warm, comfortable feeling in my heart whenever I was around Ann.

6

Run

It was summer, and once again I attended day camp in the city park. I enjoyed being with other kids and with the friendly counselors, and had my first taste of Kool-Aid. My counselors took the fine colored powder and shook it up in water. *I wonder if it's like Crystal Light that comes in the little plastic cups?* I thought. I liked sneaking dry Crystal Light at home, dipping my wet finger into it and then licking my finger. Mom always said the powder was too strong, so she never poured a whole Crystal Light cup into a pitcher of water. When my counselor handed me a styrofoam cup of Kool-Aid, I hesitated, wondering if drinking it was worth the risk of being struck by Mom; you could never know when she might turn up on the scene, as she had at school that day of the sucker, or how she might find out after the fact. But I was so very thirsty! It was over a hundred degrees outside, and we were outside all day; even in the shade, under the trees, we were dripping with sweat. It was still hours before I would go home. I quickly gulped down the Kool-Aid and prayed that my tongue wouldn't stay bright red. I knew by the taste that I could never let Mom know I'd had even a sip of the red stuff.

I kept trying to look down at my own tongue. Mom always checked the color of my tongue to see if I had eaten any candy. I was so thirsty! I wasn't used to the taste of the Kool-Aid, and didn't even really like it, but it was sweltering outside and I wanted to quench my thirst.

When several of my friends got up to walk to the restrooms on the other side of the park, I decided to go along.

"I need to go too," I called after them. We were not allowed to walk alone between the campsite and the restrooms, but upon arriving I saw there was no more toilet paper, so I ran back to the campsite to grab some. By the time I had returned to the bathrooms, my friends had all left. *I'll just hurry and catch up,* I said to myself. I was sitting on the toilet when I heard a loud crash against the stone wall of the bathroom. As the sound echoed through the concrete walls, I quickly finished my business and walked out. I saw a large man outside, and as we locked eyes he began to run toward me. I knew in my heart that something was terribly wrong, and I too began to run. I heard the words of the nurse from the hospital echoing in my heart, "You will run so fast again one day," and God seemed to whisper over and over in my ear, "Run, run, run, run, Estella!" I tossed my head as I ran. My feet were swift, my legs stretching rapidly over chunks of green lawn, and I didn't feel the familiar pain in my side. Looking over my shoulder, I saw that the heavyset man was still running after me.

He is so fat, he will never catch up to me, I thought. Wiry and thin, especially after my appendectomy, I had little weight to carry; I was not short, and yet weighed only fifty-five pounds. I had healed from the surgery, and I was fast! I continued to run, and this time I didn't look back. As soon as I arrived at the campsite I told the counselors, and the police were called. Looking on as the man was handcuffed, I noticed beer cans and a gun on the dashboard of his car. I knew that God had protected me that day.

That night I thanked the Lord as I realized there had been no trouble about my red tongue. I had forgotten all about it, but either the redness had disappeared, or Mom simply did not notice; I wasn't sure which. I flipped open my Bible. I was reading straight through the Old Testament and was at 1 Kings 18. My jaw dropped as I came to the end of the chapter, verse 46: "Then the hand of the Lord was on Elijah, and he girded up his loins and outran Ahab to Jezreel." *Wow! I outran that man today. It must have been you running inside me, Lord, just like with Elijah! First you are a nurse, and now you are a runner.* I was awed by God's provision. He was true to his Word.

Shortly after that, Mom and Dad became foster parents.

"Some children are abused by their parents and have to be taken away for a while," Mom explained. "During that time, the children stay with foster parents who will take better care of them until the real parents change. A little boy is soon to come into our home. He was burned with cigarettes."

My eyes widened. I couldn't imagine being burned with cigarettes. How horrible.

I had always wanted a little baby brother or sister. My brother was so close in age to me, he was more like a friend, not someone to hold and cuddle and make laugh. I loved telling stories to Audrey, the little girl I babysat. I would tell this little boy stories, too, and would love all his burn marks away. How could anyone burn a precious little child? The irony of this abused boy being sent to our home as a haven was lost on me at the time.

Our foster boy arrived, and so did summer. We often packed the car and took off for the Ranch, about five hours away. I had more freedom at the Ranch, where we were allowed to roam for hours across the countryside. There was a house on the property, built in the early 1900s, and leading up to the house was a dirt road. Halfway between the bump gate and the Ranch house was a dam filled with water that spilled over a concrete wall and ran into the creek, forming little pools of water here and there. We kids loved romping through the creek, splashing and getting wet in the hot summer sun. To the south of the dam was a canyon small enough that we could climb its walls. Water streamed down through the clay rock, into other little creekbeds. And if we came at just the right time, the fields were covered with flowers, beautiful bluebonnets and yellow daisies. I loved being at the Ranch, but our carefree days there were hampered by Mom's presence. *Why does she have to come?* I thought. *She only complains about the long five-hour car ride.*

One day at the Ranch we kids walked into the house from our afternoon hike. I was famished, but it was too risky to sneak food right now, with Mom close by; I would wait until she was outside or in the bathroom. I walked through the creaky old house, from the back door to the front where there was a porch swing. We sometimes got a little wild on the porch swing; it was a lot of fun. I looked at our little foster child, who was about six years old and seemed to be enjoying himself. He was with us for quite a few months.

How could anyone burn this cute little boy? I thought again to myself. Suddenly, I felt a jerk.

"Mom, what's wrong?"

"Don't say a word," she replied. I didn't even know what I had done or what this was about. "Clark!" she stormed at Dad. "Take Estella outside and hold her till I get there." Then she dashed off into the yard. What the heck was she doing now? It surely couldn't be good for me.

"This is for your own good, Estella," declared Mom. "Now, Clark," she said, handing Dad a switch she had carefully selected from the hillside, "whip Estella with this." Dad did as he was told. He always did exactly as she said, without question. Mom mumbled something to him about what I had done, but I couldn't hear. After Dad finished, it was Mom's turn to whip me.

I never did learn what it was I had done wrong. Later I sat outside in a sprawling cedar tree, listening to the cooing of the mourning doves. They always seemed to echo my sadness. I remembered a verse I had read, Jeremiah 14:19. "We looked for peace, but there was no good; and for the time of healing, and there was trouble." I became engrossed with the soft, beautiful sound of the doves as they echoed each other, and my mind darted back to a familiar Scripture that I had memorized as a song, John 14:27. "Peace I leave with you, my peace I give to you; not as the world gives do I give to you. Let not your heart be troubled, neither let it be afraid." I sang the words again and again until I felt my heart encouraged and peace began to flood my inmost being. The happiness I found in little pleasures at home or school always seemed tainted, but the peace I had in Jesus could never be taken away from me; even in the most bitter circumstances, I could hope in him because he gave not as my mother gave, not as my father gave, not as the world gave.

Jesus gives one hundred percent of himself and never takes back.

Encouraged, I stood up and walked confidently toward the Ranch house. Once inside, I would pretend with Mom that nothing had happened. That's the way she liked it.

7

Loss

I was now nearing my tenth birthday, and fifth grade was approaching. Things did not seem well between Granny (Dad's mother) and my mom. I was standing in the kitchen, and Mom and Dad were arguing. Well, actually, Mom was arguing at Dad; Dad couldn't seem to get a word in edgewise.

"You pick! Either your mother or me!" barked Mom. "I want our phone number changed, too, to one that no one else knows. I want a private number so no one can call here anymore, especially your mother!"

"Okay, Donna, whatever you say," replied my father gingerly.

I turned to leave the kitchen and went back to my room, hoping Mom would not notice I had left. I had a special Holly Hobby tea set that Mom had passed down to me, and I set up a grand tea party for all my Cabbage Patch and

Raggedy Ann and Andy dolls. Sitting on the carpet with them all gathered around, I noticed the warm summer sun shining through my yellow curtains, soft and inviting. I climbed up on the sill of my bay window and twisted the slats of the mini-blinds down so that the sun would shine directly onto my face. The warmth felt good and I forgot about everything else for a moment. Then I looked back at the tea party spread out on the carpet, and hopped back down to join my dolls.

After that day I wasn't allowed to see much of Granny, Aunt Jean and Uncle Teddy, or the rest of Dad's family, except on special holidays, and even then our visits were always supervised. We weren't allowed to be alone with any family much, especially those who lived close by. At Thanksgiving we all went to Granny and Grampy's house. I was allowed a piece of pumpkin pie, but forbidden to eat the crust.

"Pumpkin pie is healthy for you, Estella. You may eat a small piece without crust, as long as you eat this potato salad first."

Oh, my gosh, not potato salad! You know how much I hate potato salad. It was almost as bad as oatmeal. She gave me a large serving just to torment me, or perhaps to punish me for some unknown crime, and watched as I ate the potato salad and then later dessert, carefully cutting away each little bit of crust. When we returned home, I felt sick to my stomach and threw up the potato salad. I couldn't understand why Mom made me eat stuff that obviously made me sick.

In fifth grade I had several teachers, all for different subjects. One in particular was stricter than the others and was greatly feared by every child in my school who had ever come near her. She never smiled, and never complimented anyone on their work. If she asked a question and no one knew the answer, she would stand aghast in disbelief at the sheer magnitude of our stupidity. "How is it possible that you do not know these very basic facts?" she would say. But I thought to myself, *Maybe she's like this because no one has ever been nice to her. I will try to win her over to kinder ways by giving her gifts. I will be nice to her, even if she appears not to like me.*

So I carefully selected some roses from our garden at home; I was in charge of the roses, and it was my job to tend them carefully every day in addition to my other morning chores. I had been sternly instructed by Mom in the right way to prune them.

"You must cut each wilted flower off right above a five leaflet and *only* a five leaflet," she commanded. *Or it will be my life,* I thought warily. I chose pink roses for my teacher and presented them to her one morning in class. She received them with great surprise, and I saw a smile cross her lips for the first time. On another day, I presented her with an apple. I was only allowed small portions myself, never a whole apple, but I had told Mom that the apple was for my teacher, not myself, and she had let me have it. The apple was well received by my teacher, and the year marched by rapidly once I'd warmed her up a little.

One day as Mom and I were driving home, we passed a house with a pomegranate tree in the yard, loaded with fruit.

"Estella, I want you to go pick some pomegranates from that yard," commanded Mom. I knew better than to argue, but I shuddered: the house was none other than that of my teacher, the one who rarely smiled and with whom I had made such an effort to win a tenuous peace. What if she caught me raiding her tree and was hard on me at school? There was only one thing to do. I would have to work up the nerve to knock on her door. I took a grocery bag and rode my bicycle to her home.

"I was wondering if I could pick some of your pomegranates," I said when the door opened.

"Sure, Estella. Help yourself," she replied cordially. I couldn't believe how simple that had been! Having completed my mission and acquired a few choice pomegranates for my mother, I rode triumphantly home on my bicycle.

Riding my bike was one of my favorite things to do besides playing the piano, and I rode it everywhere. I loved babysitting, too. I had started when I was nine years old and now I had grown quite attached to the kids I babysat. I loved hugging the little girl I often cared for, and liked fixing her hair, telling her stories, and playing with her in her family's backyard. I enjoyed it all a little too much, though; Mom had noticed how much I liked babysitting, and had begun to use it manipulatively against me. Anything I really enjoyed, I was always in danger of losing; taking beloved things away from me was Mom's secret weapon. To make matters worse, I always managed to find food wherever I babysat; it was one of the ways I fed myself, and perhaps Mom knew this. If denied the privilege by Mom, I would miss babysitting *and* eating. I hated always being hungry and feeling like I was doing something wrong by eating. I struggled with feelings of guilt about the food I ate surreptitiously, as Mom and Dad had always stressed the importance of obedience and truthfulness.

Placing the pomegranates on the counter in front of Mom, I brought my thoughts back to the situation at hand. I always had to be wary, on my toes, around Mom.

"Estella, you may babysit if you complete this list of chores. First you must scrub the baseboards in the kitchen with a toothbrush. You must then dust off all the silk plants with a damp cloth. Be sure and take the Dustbuster and vacuum the ceiling, especially all the corners. After that, I want you to dust all the table and chair legs, being sure to get inside each little crack. I will check your work at the end of the week, and if it is satisfactory, you may babysit," said Mom.

I confidently informed the family down the street that I would be able to babysit next time they needed me. On the day of the babysitting job, I had already completed all the required tasks and it was getting to be time for me to go down the street. I wondered, with agitation, if Mom even remembered that this was the day I was supposed to babysit. I hated to bring it up. The more I thought about mentioning it to her, the more fearful I became. I thought, with each passing hour, *I will remind Mom in the next hour that I'm supposed to babysit today.* But hour after hour passed as I kept waiting for an opportune moment or any sign of a good mood from Mom's direction.

Finally, the critical hour arrived. I had put it off long enough. It was now almost time for me to leave, or I would be late to my job. I slipped away to my bedroom to braid my hair and make sure I looked nice, resolving to broach the babysitting subject with Mom as soon as I was ready.

"Where do you think you're going?" asked Mom.

"I'm going to babysit. Is that okay?" I replied. "I finished all the work you assigned me."

"Young lady, do think you are going anywhere with the kitchen like this? Look! You left the radio out of place in the center of the kitchen cabinet. You should have pushed it back up against the wall once I was done listening to my radio programs. Also, this jar lid is still out. You should have put it away. You are not going anywhere tonight!"

I stood in shocked amazement. I knew Mom was unpredictable and arbitrary, but I suppose I avoided giving way to despair by hovering in a constant state of denial. My heart fell. I had looked forward to this night all week! For days I had waited, looking forward to a chance to get out of the house, and now on top of not going anywhere I would have to suffer the humiliation of having to cancel the job at the last moment. I knew this was very unprofessional. *How mortifying,* I thought.

This began to happen more and more with any activity I enjoyed: going to a friend's place to spend the night, going roller skating at the rink, or even just riding my bicycle down the street to my friend's house for a little bit of free time were all subject to being forbidden by Mom on the slightest pretext. I had always been allowed to ride my bicycle all over the neighborhood, and would visit everyone within riding distance; I was the social butterfly of the neighborhood. I was also the number one seller of Girl Scout cookies, going door to door with my brochure. I lived for these little outings, and every time there was a chance of going out, I would work hard to complete the required tasks. So many times my hopes were dashed—but not always. Sometimes, in her capriciousness, my mom would let me go. I was the eternal optimist, and my enthusiasm never waned.

"Why do you even bother getting all excited every time you think you're going to get to go somewhere?" commented my brother. "You get all happy and excited, and then you are just disappointed."

"I would rather anticipate fun and be happy for a little while, and be disappointed, than never be happy or excited at all," I snapped in rebuttal. I knew that I had to have something to look forward to in life.

That year, I had a very unexpected and pleasant surprise. My parents were still part of the foster care system. We had taken in two children before, and they had touched my heart. I had always wanted a baby brother or baby sister of my own. Now I returned home from school one day to find a new little person waiting for my care: Shiloh, a little girl nine months old. Oh, how I loved her with every bit of my heart! I held her as often as I could, and rocked her every evening before putting her to bed; she never wanted to go to bed, and would cry for thirty minutes every night after I laid her down. I would sing to her, and I was always the one who got up in the middle of the night to give her a bottle.

Mom seemed more docile while my little baby doll Shiloh was with us. It didn't take long for me to get very attached. I hated leaving her during the day to go to school, but it was so wonderful to have something to look forward to at home every day! Instead of the usual dread, I felt warm love filling my heart for this precious little girl. Loving and caring for her soothed the pain in my own heart that I was accustomed to feeling every day.

It was Friday now, and I was looking forward to the weekend with Shiloh. She had been with us for just one week, but to me it felt like an eternity already because of its powerful effect on my outlook and because I had come to love her so much. I took the bus across town to a parking lot where Dad met me to drive me the rest of the way home. I skipped lightly up the sidewalk toward my dad, but when I reached him I saw a sad look in his eyes. At home we pulled slowly into the long driveway that wrapped around the back of the house, and drove into the garage. I took my shoes off as I reached the back door, and Dad began saying something.

I couldn't believe my ears. Dad was explaining to me how Shiloh's grandmother had come and taken her away. I just couldn't understand. It wasn't fair! I hadn't even had a chance to say goodbye! What right did the grandmother have to just come and take her? If she had wanted Shiloh so badly, why hadn't she taken her in the first place? I wanted to say all of this, but I bit my tongue. Hot tears welled up in my eyes, but I forced them back. I just couldn't cry right now; I had to think about Mom and what this would do to her. She had really enjoyed Shiloh. So had Dad.

Later that night I cried myself to sleep as the shock of what happened began to wear off. I almost couldn't believe that she was really gone and I hadn't even been able to say goodbye. I resented the fact that my parents hadn't come to pick me up early from school once they had realized Shiloh was leaving us. How could they be so heartless?

I remembered what Job, in the Old Testament, had said when he lost his loved ones. I couldn't let anyone know that I was still up, so I clicked on my flashlight underneath the sheet as I cracked open my Bible to read Job 1:21. "And he said, 'Naked I came from my mother's womb, and naked shall I return there. The Lord gave, and the Lord has taken away; blessed be the name of the Lord.'" Somehow, as awful as those words seemed, I felt a little better. I was not the only one who suffered.

"Lord Jesus," I prayed, "please get me through this time of losing someone I love so much. I felt like Shiloh was my little sister, and now she's gone forever. I'll never see her again, and worst of all, I didn't even get to say goodbye." Tears splashed onto the thin, worn pages of my Bible. Sobbing, I clutched the open Bible to my heart. "Lord, I'm so disappointed because I thought Shiloh would get to stay with us for a very long time. They said she would stay for almost a year, at least six months! How could this happen?" Finally sleep overcame me, and before I knew it morning had come and I was back to the same drudgery I faced every day: countless household chores done in the knowledge that no matter how hard I tried, Mom would still fly off the handle.

The months marched on. Now here I stood, outside on our retaining wall, reflecting on the long years that had passed. I often stood on the retaining wall, looking out over the town while I talked to Jesus as the sun set. I loved watching our beautiful Texan sunsets; our front yard offered a panorama of the entire town and miles beyond. The open space gave such a sense of freedom! It was refreshing to be outside for a few moments. I balanced along the towering brick wall, remembering the balance beam at my gymnastics program. Mom and Dad had hit hard times, so gymnastics was a thing of the past now. I would still have my piano, ballet, and choirs at church, though.

My contemplations were suddenly interrupted by a loud explosion. Huge clouds of smoke began to rise at the other end of town, not far from my school, and I could make out flames as they leapt into the air. I sat and watched and wondered as billow after billow of dark, dense smoke somersaulted into the air. The next day I climbed the steps of the bus with my friend. I liked her very much, but didn't get to see much of her because she wasn't in my home classroom.

"Did you hear the explosion? Did you see the fire at the north end of town yesterday?" I asked her excitedly.

"Yes; that was my dad," she replied. My feet froze on the steps of the bus. I couldn't think of anything to say. My heart was crushed for my friend. I had lost Shiloh without saying goodbye, but she had lost her father forever. The bus driver motioned for me to continue into the vehicle, and I managed to climb the remaining steps and find a seat. I couldn't imagine losing a father like that. As we sat together on the bus, I looked with sadness into my friend's eyes. She wouldn't say much else, and I felt helpless to comfort her.

I was daily dealing with my own grief and was rarely allowed to meet with friends; if she wouldn't talk to me at school, then I couldn't help her except through prayer.

8

Muffins

My school day usually ended with bell choir or music class.
There was one boy in particular who really got on my
nerves, especially in bell choir. He was always annoying me.
Well, today I had decided I would annoy him! In bell choir
class I teased and pestered him mercilessly. My teacher kept
telling me to stop, but I just wanted to enact simple justice:
life seemed so unfair sometimes! How come this kid could
annoy me constantly and never get in trouble? Not that I
ever got in trouble at school myself. But this time I heard
words I had never heard before.

"Estella, go to the principal's office," ordered my teacher.

"But... but... but," I stammered.

"Go, Estella."

I had never before endured this humiliation. It was made
worse by the fact that the principal was a friend of my family.

I was dead meat for sure! I couldn't face going to the principal's office, so I fled into the girls' bathroom; since bell choir was my last class, I could stay in the bathroom until it was time to get into the bus line. When I heard the last bell of the day, I slipped out of the bathroom and into the long line of kids preparing to board the bus.

The principal came up to me and whispered, "Estella, we are never going to do that again, are we?"

I shook my head silently, and she walked off. I breathed a sigh of relief. I could not take such a risk ever again; if Mom found out, she would kill me for sure. I climbed aboard the bus, suffocated by the fumes, and wished I weren't going home. The worst part was the long, smoggy bus ride, thinking about my foolish behavior and worrying about what would happen. But the school year came to a close without my principal ever breathing a word to my parents of what had happened that day. Little did she know the great favor she did me by keeping it to herself! I would be eternally grateful.

Months passed and the school year was over. I looked forward to riding my bike to Audrey's house and babysitting her, having missed doing that while I was in school. When I wasn't babysitting, Gabriel and I were romping the Mountain during our free time; we were allowed free time for two hours after the heat of the day was past, but were forbidden to go outside before four o'clock in the afternoon.

"The sun isn't good for you," Mom always declared.

One day, as usual, I prepared a little lunch for all of us—under the direction of Mom, of course; I had all the household responsibilities beneath her scrutinizing eye. We had tuna fish that day: one can of tuna, packed in water, to be divided amongst the four of us. No salt or pepper or even mayo was allowed, because that was considered unhealthy. I had been told to mix the tuna with half a chopped onion and a little yogurt to make up for the missing mayo, and to smear the tuna mixture onto four small bits of pita bread. The wet tuna made the pita bread soggy, so that my tuna kept falling out of the bottom of my bit of pita. The wet, mushy bread felt gross in my mouth, but I didn't dare give up a meal.

With dishes done and put away, rooms cleaned, and bathroom spotless, Gabriel and I were free to roam. Agile and eager, I charged up the hillside littered with cactus and cedar, practicing my sprints, and Gabriel followed as we headed off to our fort. We had just finished building it, nailing boards across tree limbs and tying rope to a sturdy branch for a little swing, and I had swept away dirt from the ground to make a little clearing. But as I passed the cistern, I heard a noise. I came to an abrupt stop and my brother crashed into me.

"Hey! Why did you stop?" he exclaimed.

"I thought I heard something, Gabriel." We inched our way towards the cistern. It was taller than I was, but I jumped up and down, catching a glimpse inside with each jump, until I could make out the source of the mysterious sound.

"What is it?" asked my brother.

"I don't know. It looks like a cross between a raccoon and a squirrel." Then I started racing back down to the house.

"Where are you going?" asked Gabriel.

"To get an animal book!" I retorted. Soon I came tromping back through the brush, armed with something to stand on and a long board.

"It's a ring-tail," I announced.

"A what?"

"A ring-tail. It must have gotten trapped." Dad came following behind me and helped us get the board inside the cistern to give the animal a way to climb out. After staring at the curious creature, Gabriel and I continued up the Mountain to our fort.

"I wonder if the ring-tail will escape, or if he will just stay in there," I mused aloud. We spent all the rest of our time that afternoon playing in our little makeshift fort. Suddenly I heard my name screamed at a blood-curdling pitch, and then Gabriel's. We fixed each other with an "Oh, my gosh" look and raced down the side of the Mountain, careening through cactus. I didn't care if I got scratched; what Mom was probably about to do to us would be even worse if we delayed, far worse than any cactus needle could inflict. We made it back to the house, breathless and in fear of what might come next.

"We're here, Mom. We came just as soon as we heard you call."

"Get in the house." Silent, I hurried into the house through the back door before Mom. I hated having her behind my back like that where I couldn't see her; if she were to lunge at me, it would take me by surprise. We hadn't been late, so I wondered what the problem could be. With Mom, there was no telling!

It turned out to be not as bad as expected. I thought about it again later that night, as I lay under my covers engrossed in my new book. I had the covers and a couple of pillows thrown over my head and was reading with a flashlight—all night. It was a risky thing to do, since Mom sometimes got up and entered my room in the middle of the night, but I just had to escape into my own world. The suspense of answering Mom's call had been the worst part of the afternoon. My crime was that I had left the phone out of place, scooted out too far on the counter when it was supposed to be right against the wall. It had made her frantic with anger, but this time, thankfully, Mom had calmed down almost as quickly as she had riled up.

Riled up: that was the word she always used with me. She said I riled her up. I didn't know how to be a way that would make her happy. I did the best I could every day and it didn't seem to be helping, but I would keep trying with all my heart every day. I didn't really have a choice; if I didn't try harder, there would be no chance of me ever going anywhere or ever getting to do anything fun. Sometimes I got to go places with Lynda, the girl Mom had hired to help around the house. Lynda was like my big sister now. She was so nice to me, and sometimes she babysat us. If Lynda took us somewhere, which wasn't very often, she would make a mad dash into a gas station to buy us candy for the play or movie or whatever it was we were about to go to.

Then one day I received great news: I was going to be homeschooled, and Lynda was going to help with our homeschooling all throughout the fall semester. To top it off, Vacation Bible School at First Baptist Church was starting. I went every day and enjoyed the extra singing, fun crafts and activities, Scripture memory contest, helping with the babies in the nursery—and snack time! VBS was my favorite part of the whole summer.

Now summer was about to end, and Mom had left for the day.

"Let's make muffins," I decided. "I'll use Mom's special cookbook from college. The one she used to teach me how to cook."

"Muffins! Are you crazy?" said Gabriel.

"Gabriel, I'm so hungry and I just want something goooood to eat for a change." So I got the cookbook out, and soon the oven was on and the muffin tins were oiled.

"Oh no! We don't have any sugar or butter in the house. Why didn't I think about that?" We both stared dumbfounded at the mess we had already created in the kitchen. Then I had an idea. "I know! I'll ask my piano teacher." I raced across the street to tell my new piano teacher that we were out of sugar and butter; could we please borrow some? In a few minutes I marched triumphantly back home with the baking ingredients, and before long the kitchen was filled with the delicious aroma of baking. When the muffins were ready, I sank my teeth into one of them and ate it slowly, savoring every bite. Then another. So did Gabriel.

"Wow, Gabriel!" I was jubilant. "We did it! These are the best muffins I've ever eaten!" We cleaned up our mess and aired out the house, and I sprayed the kitchen down with a strong cleanser. I had to clean the kitchen anyway as one of my chores, and Mom was going to be gone a long time, so she would be none the wiser. It would be fine. Afterward, we brushed our teeth. I smiled in the mirror as I checked my teeth. Mom would check our tongues and teeth as soon as she got home to make sure we hadn't eaten anything.

"I'm full. I actually feel full, Gabriel," I said happily after gargling with hydrogen peroxide as an extra precaution.

"Me too," mumbled Gabriel as he swabbed his teeth.

Later, Mom came home from running errands and attending her club event.

"Did you finish the list of chores I left for you to do?" she asked.

"Yes, and I swept and mopped the floor just like you said."

"Well, let's just have a look and see." She marched into the kitchen. It almost sparkled with cleanliness.

"You missed some dirt with the broom, Estella." Stifling a sigh, I picked up the broom and resumed cleaning yet again—something I had grown accustomed to because of Mom's infinite perfectionism. It wasn't even dirt, actually; it was really just lint. After mopping, little films of dirt sometimes collected here and there, and I had forgotten about that.

"Now get on your hands and knees and clean up the rest," she added. Already my wonderful day was over. Once again, I was waiting for her to leave.

9

From Hell to Paradise

My eleventh birthday came, and with it a new school year.
I enjoyed doing school on my own and with Lynda. I felt a
little safer with Lynda around, knowing that Mom would
be more careful around her, at least to a certain extent.
She would not be quite so severe. Still, some things never
changed. Mom would still feed me the oatmeal, then stand
over me and repeat the spiel about what a disobedient and
horrible child I was.

She turned to Lynda and said, "This oatmeal thing is
always a battle with her. It's always a battle. She keeps
fighting me on this oatmeal thing." A week passed, and one
night I cried out to God.

"Lord, I can't take another day of stomach cramps. It
hurts so bad, but Mom will make me eat the oatmeal again
tomorrow. What do I do, Lord? I can't endure another

morning like this," I prayed. I waited on the Lord to answer my question. I loved lying in bed, thinking and praying after reading my Bible every night. As I lay there, the Lord answered me.

"Eat lemon, and it will help your stomach digest the food."

The next morning Dad woke me up before six o'clock to start my morning chores. Sure enough, oatmeal was simmering in the pot. I took a lemon, sliced it up, and ate a couple of pieces. My stomach almost cramped just at the thought of eating the oatmeal, but I had high hopes for the outcome of God's word to me. I swallowed the lemon, all except the seeds and peel.

"What are you doing?" snapped Mom. I jumped.

"I'm eating lemon with the oatmeal so it won't make me sick," I replied.

"Oh. Okay." Miraculously, she said nothing more, but turned and walked over to my dad. It was almost time for Lynda to arrive for the day, and a few minutes later she walked through the door. Dad shot a worried glance in her direction and then murmured something to Mom that I couldn't make out. I stared at the remaining pieces of lemon, then gulped them down quickly before Mom could change her mind about letting me eat them. I hadn't even asked her!

It worked. Oatmeal would never make me sick again! After that day, I always consumed my lemon slices before the rough oatmeal dish, and Mom never said a word about it. God had heard my cry and answered me that day. My heart filled with longing to know God more. He had made it clear that he loved me, even if my own parents did not.

Much later, when hunger drove me to sneak raw oats and I ate them with no ill effects, I figured that Mom must have been deliberately adding something to my oatmeal that upset my stomach, and that Lynda had observed her doing so when she came in that day; that must have been why Dad had been uneasy and had made that quiet aside to Mom. Perhaps it was not the lemon that had made the difference after all; perhaps it was that Mom had stopped adding whatever it was to my oatmeal once she knew Lynda suspected. Either way, though, God had answered my prayer.

Every day, while Lynda cleaned and did paperwork, I had to sit in the master bathroom and read history and science to Mom while she took her bath. Sometimes that was good: it seemed as if Mom almost enjoyed talking to me, and I felt a measure of safety while I was reading.

But then one day I was shocked to hear the family news flash: Mom was moving to Lubbock again for the spring semester, only this time she was taking me with her. Why would she take *me* with her? She didn't even love me; she loved Gabriel. The only explanation was that she couldn't stand to let me out from under her watchful gaze, even for a few months. I was devastated. I would have to leave Lynda and Gabriel—and Dad. Dad was the only one who loved me. Mom had been better for a while after my surgery, but once I had fully recovered she had worsened to a state more violent than before. I just couldn't understand why she would want me with her. The only saving grace of the situation was that I was to be placed in a very good school in Lubbock.

Later that day, I stood in my bedroom trembling as Mom brandished the whip over my head. The bedroom door was open a crack, and Lynda passed by. I looked down in utter humiliation and embarrassment. Mom hadn't even noticed Lynda.

Soon I was left alone with the terrifying thought of living alone with my mom. Without Dad around at all, and no Lynda to ease my pain, I wondered how I would survive. Sneaking food would be harder, too. Sometimes I snuck graham crackers and other snacks when I was hungry; there was always a bitter price to pay, but at the time it always seemed worth it. How would I feed myself in Lubbock? If any food disappeared there, Mom would know instantly that I was the culprit. I would just have to play it by ear. I didn't want Lynda to see me upset and in tears, but I was never allowed to shut any door for privacy, so I hibernated in the closet beneath my hanging clothes until my eyes were dry.

Sixth grade in Lubbock was my last good experience of school, but it was mixed with bitter tears. I made new friends there, and although I was allowed to hang out with them only on their birthdays, it was still a blessing and a great relief during that spring. Also, I was placed in Honor Choir at school, and we competed in a prestigious music festival and won first place. I had many different teachers, all of whom were very kind. I liked one particular teacher the best, my Reading teacher. She was sick a lot though, from cancer, and this resulted in us having many substitute teachers. *Why do I always have to get attached to people who go away?* I thought. My homeroom teacher was very good too, and my Science teacher was hilariously serious. She spoke multiple languages. One day a student cussed at her in Spanish, and to his surprise she answered back in Spanish. The look on that boy's face was priceless!

I went into the school weighing only about fifty-five pounds; I had gained no weight for the last four years. After eating lunch every day in the cafeteria, I started to gain weight. The food here was so much better than the food at my last school, and the portions were larger. I was still hungry, though. The food at school was really all I got. I had to make it through the nights at the apartment on the fullness of lunch alone. I would try to snack during the afternoon using the quarters I had scrounged for the vending machines, but sometimes I would get caught eating in class; my homeroom teacher was a little more lenient than the others, and would usually let me off with just a warning, but the others were stricter. Saving my snack to eat on the bus was not an option, either, because Mom would be sure to check my mouth as soon as I walked through the door. If there was even a hint of junk food or candy on my breath, my life would be over.

At the end of each day I boarded the bus for the apartment complex. Other kids would always be talking about movies they had seen, movies that I would never watch. *How could kids watch those horror shows?* I thought. I wanted to fill my mind with God every second that I could, because I knew that I needed the Lord above anything else. He was the only one who was going to help me get through each evening with Mom. I had to walk from one side of the apartment complex, where the bus dropped me off, to the other side, where our apartment was. I would slowly put one foot in front of the other, dreading each and every step, but I was afraid to walk too slowly, because then Mom would get upset that I was late. I felt each step like the piercings of a million poisoned arrows into my feet. It made me think of the story of the Little Mermaid: after she got the legs she had longed for, she always felt as if she were walking on

I went to school weighing only 55 pounds.

glass, and bled with each step. I dreaded each step like that! The difference was that I hadn't asked for this life, and I wasn't bleeding, so no one would ever know the suffering I was enduring. I fixed my mind on Psalm 23: "Yea, though I walk through the valley of the shadow of death, I will fear no evil, for thou art with me." I was thinking of it this day as I stepped through the door of the apartment.

"I'm home, Mom," I called out. No sweet smile met me at the door, but then, I never expected one. I dropped my books on the stale-looking brown carpet in my room and flopped onto the bed. I needed to study for my upcoming Science test. Mom was probably doing her own studying in the other room. After all, that's why we were there in Lubbock, so that she could finish getting her degree in Hotel, Restaurant, and Institutional Management. *She must still be studying for her Sanitation class,* I thought. After an hour of study, Mom called to me from the living room.

"Estella, the living room carpet needs to be vacuumed."

"OK, I'll get right on it," I said. Mom stood over me as I pushed the vacuum cleaner back and forth.

"The lines left by the vacuum cleaner must be perfectly straight," she reminded me.

I grasped the clumsy appliance more firmly and pushed it forward, then brought it straight back, being careful to go back over the same vacuum line I had just created. I began to shake, like I always did when Mom was close to me. I didn't dare look, but I knew she was standing close by. Nervousness seized me. My mind darted to Isaiah 21:3: "Therefore my loins are filled with pain; pangs have taken hold of me like the pangs of a woman in labor... My heart wavered, and fearfulness frightened me." I couldn't wait for nighttime when I would be allowed to go to bed and get some relief! In my mind, lying in bed, I could take myself wherever I wanted to be before I fell asleep.

Suddenly I felt a powerful thump against my back. My body fell forward, but I caught myself on the vacuum cleaner.

"Estella, you just hit the furniture! Look at the white mark on the table leg." The table leg was already in bad shape; Mom had furnished the apartment with old, used cheap stuff. The vacuum was old too, and very cumbersome, bigger and heavier than I was. I could hardly push it today.

"Estella, you're not staying in the lines when you pull back on the vacuum cleaner. How many times do I have to stand over you and check your work?"

"Yes, Ma'am."

"Move the table and vacuum under it."

"Yes, Ma'am."

"Get the attachment out and vacuum around the couch legs. Make sure you get every little speck of dirt. Do you hear?"

"Yes, Ma'am." Mom slapped me across the face.

"Stop shaking and flinching. How many times have I told you to stop flinching?"

"Yes, Ma'am." I thought of Psalm 23 again. I knew God was with me. I breathed in and let my mind go to nighttime. The day couldn't last forever; eventually, she would want to go to bed. I was just about finished with the vacuuming when suddenly I felt a squeeze around my arm. I winced in pain as all five of Mom's fingernails dug into the tender flesh of my bicep. My body was jerked sideways and I half followed, half fell after Mom as she dragged me into the kitchen. She punched the microwave door release button, and I flinched again at the sharp sound.

"Look at the microwave. Just look at the microwave! I told you to clean this after breakfast, this morning, before you left to catch the bus! See all the lint you left behind. After you used the sponge, you should have used Windex and paper towel. Now fix it!" I caught up a fresh paper towel into my hand and reached for the Windex as Mom loosened her grip on my arm. I would fix this quickly, and then maybe she would forget how upset she was.

"Ahhhh!" Mom screamed. "I told you not to go through too many paper towels in one day! Where is the piece you saved from earlier this morning?" I glanced frantically around the small kitchen. My eyes darted toward the trash can. "Is it in the *trash*?" she shrieked. Another slap across my face. Quickly, I spotted the used paper towel near the sink.

"Here it is, Mom. I've got it. See, it wasn't in the trash." I quickly turned to reach into the microwave, but I was too late. Mom slapped me again, and this time my head bounced off the half-open microwave door. "I'll fix it right away, right away," I said desperately, and started to scrub at the inside of the microwave as my face became marred with tears. I went over and over the inside, but the paper towel seemed to be fraying. How could I keep the lint from getting all over the microwave? I tried with every ounce of my being to get the inside clean, but it seemed hopeless.

"There is still a smudge on the inside of the door," declared Mom. I tried harder. Finally, I finished the inside.

"Now you need to buff the outside." My ragged paper towel was starting to wear through, so I picked up an old rag towel. My parents had money and very nice things; I didn't understand why we couldn't use better cloth rags and more paper towels. Mom never liked throwing anything away. She saved everything, and always made me use the oldest and most used of everything. After thirty minutes of cleaning, I finished the microwave to her satisfaction. I felt exhausted, but it was too early to go to bed. Mom would never let me off that easy.

"Now you need to go polish the vacuum marks off the furniture in the other room. Go," she said, giving me a shove. But then, confusingly, she grabbed a potato and chucked it into my hands.

"It's time for dinner now. I'm going to cook a potato. Wash this, poke holes in it, and then microwave it for several minutes. Make sure it doesn't explode," Mom ordered, fixing me with a penetrating glare. She had the most fearsome pair of eyeballs I had ever seen. I felt uncertain: should I work on the furniture or the potato? I continued on to the living room, and after several minutes of careful buffing I turned my attention to the potato in the kitchen. After the potato was done, Mom cut a small piece off the end of it for my dinner. Butter, salt, and sour cream were not allowed.

"Unhealthy," she always declared. "You may put a little non-fat, sugar-free yogurt on it if you wish." Yogurt was Mom's answer to every food issue. I ate my little bit of potato and wondered how much longer the evening could last. My mind went to one of my favorite hymns: "The Solid Rock." The words whirled through my mind:

> My hope is built on nothing less
> than Jesus' blood and righteousness.
> I dare not trust the sweetest frame,
> but wholly lean on Jesus' name.
> On Christ the solid Rock I stand,
> all other ground is sinking sand.

Evening came. Mom had settled down and left me to bathe and get ready for bed. Bathing was the only time I was allowed to shut a door for privacy; locking it, however, was forbidden. After my bath I was finally able to curl up under the covers and read my Bible, just like I did every night. I wondered how people survived without God.

"Lord, I need you. I need you tonight, Lord." Grabbing my Bible, I let it fall open and looked down as my eyes fell on Psalm 66:12: "You have caused men to ride over our heads; we went through fire and through water; but you brought us to a place of abundance." I felt a calm assurance that eventually, someday, this awful dread would be behind me.

For now, God was my Rock. Another song popped into my head:

> I will call upon the Lord,
> who is worthy to be praised.
> So shall I be saved from my enemies;
> I will call upon the Lord.
> The Lord liveth, and blessed be my Rock,
> and may the God of my salvation be exalted.

I fell asleep as I thought of God defeating my own enemies.

The next day I felt very hungry. The evening before had left me frazzled and tense, as I never knew when Mom might get enraged about something. Another day of refreshment at school would inevitably come to an end, to be followed by the long, dreadful walk back to the apartment. I had managed to get my hands on a couple of quarters for the snack machine by selling my school supplies. Reading class began, and I waited for an opportunity to sneak a bite or two.

"Class, please take out the book *Island of the Blue Dolphins*, and turn to page..."

I tried slipping a little bit of food into my mouth. But that day I was not as lucky as usual.

"Estella," said my teacher, summoning me out into the hall, "I've warned you many times not to eat food in class. This time I'm going to send a note home to your mother, and you must get her to sign it and then return it to me." We were standing at my locker; there was no one else around. As the Reading teacher pressed the note into my hand, I burst into tears. I tried to stop crying, but the tears kept coming.

"Estella, why are you crying over this?" My teacher gazed at me in puzzlement, but I couldn't stop crying and couldn't answer her. Things were already so bad with Mom, but I never imagined something like this happening. "Estella, why are you crying? Why are you so upset over just this? Is something wrong at home?"

I thought for the longest few seconds of my life, staring down at the cold hard floor beneath my feet. If I ever told anyone what home was like, Mom would kill me.

I shook my head. No, there were no problems at home; I would give the letter to my mother. The punishment I would receive over the details of the letter wouldn't be as bad as what I would get if I told my teacher what my mom was like at home.

I gave her the letter on Friday when we were traveling home to Vulture Valley, and upon our arrival was belted by my dad as Mom watched. I hadn't seen my dad for a long time, and now I was too humiliated to look him in the eye. Instead of relief and pleasure at seeing him, I couldn't wait for the weekend to be over so I could go back to school. Life had such strange twist and turns! It seemed the only secure place for my hopes, any hope, was with God.

The school year ended. I had been placed in all advanced classes for the next year, and all my teachers asked for me to return. Mom thought about moving to Lubbock for good, but decided against it: from now on, my brother and I were to be homeschooled back in Vulture Valley. I knew life would never be the same. I had inched up from fifty-five pounds to seventy pounds just from eating once a day at school, my first weight gain since age eight. I was almost twelve now, and some people told me I looked like a mere seven-year-old. *I wonder if I... if we... will ever get to eat real food again,* I thought anxiously. Then I recalled the Scripture my Sunday

School teacher had kindly printed out for me: "Be anxious for nothing, but in everything make your requests known to God with prayer and thanksgiving. Philippians 4:6."

At the end of that hellish semester in Lubbock, something wonderful happened. I had applied to attend a Gifted and Talented program at Texas Tech University that summer, and my principal had written me a glowing letter of recommendation. I had submitted recommendations from my piano teacher and other teachers as well, and an essay on why I wanted to attend the program. I could hardly believe my ears when I was accepted and Mom told me I would be living in a college dorm for two weeks.

Thanks, God, for coming through for me, I prayed that night. I would get relief for a whole two weeks! I could hardly believe it! I was excited when the time came to pack my bags and go. Upon my arrival at the two-week camp, I met several of the other kids, all of whom were friendly. A few of them asked me why I had two black eyes. I looked at my face in the mirror.

"I didn't know I had two black eyes," I declared to the other girls standing in my dorm room.

"Well, just look. See the black circles under your eyes?"

"Yeah, I see them. Wow. I can't believe it. I never noticed," I said out loud. But I thought to myself, *It's because of Mom and how stressful it is to be around her all the time.* I hardly ever got any sleep. I was surprised Mom let me walk out in public with eyes like this; she was always so paranoid about that kind of stuff. Well, I didn't have to think about Mom for a whole two weeks now. We headed off to the cafeteria, and my eyes widened as I saw all the food.

"You mean to tell me that this card around my neck means I can eat whatever I want, three times a day?"

"Yeah, I guess so. That's what the counselor told me."

I had never seen so much food in all my life. Mom was a million miles away and there was no one to check my breath or teeth. God had heard my cry! Sheer heaven was in plain sight. I chatted with my friends at the table as we settled in, and after dinner and orientation, I played on the grand piano in the lobby. A boy walked by and turned his hat upside down on the lid of the piano as I continued to play, and people passing by dropped money in the hat. I had been told that at the end of the week we would get to take a trip to the mall, and I was so looking forward to spending my own money. I never got to go shopping. What a treat that would be! Other kids flocked to the piano. We swapped sheet music and all enjoyed playing something different out of somebody else's collection.

I soon found out that my counselor was an old dance teacher of my mine. She had, at one time, been a counselor to me in another town during a day camp program. I felt so blessed by God to be interacting with her again, someone I knew and was comfortable with. I soon discovered that her birthday was during our two weeks of camp, and since we had free time in the evenings, I decided to hold a surprise party for her in the open room at the end of the hall. No one ever used that room. I had formed quick attachments with other girls my age, and we were all in the spare room together decorating and getting ready for the party; I was hanging up streamers and blowing up balloons with the others. As I blew air into a balloon and looked down at it hanging out of my mouth, everything suddenly went black.

I seemed to be on my knees on the side of the street, with cars whizzing past me. I didn't recognize the area. Where was I? It was so dark! I opened my eyes and looked up at everyone staring down at me.

"Who are you?" I asked, bewildered. "Where am I?" I was on the carpet in the spare party room. Looking around uncertainly, I thought, *How did I get here, and where did all these people come from?*

"Who are you?" I asked again. One of the girls darted quickly from the room and returned minutes later with an adult.

"We don't know what happened to her," someone said. "She just fell and hit her head against the wall, and then kinda bounced off the wall and hit her head on the couch there, and then against the floor. Her eyes were open the whole entire time, and now she doesn't remember any of us."

"My eyes were open?" I asked in disbelief. By now I thought maybe I had been dreaming, but people didn't dream with their eyes open.

"Your eyes were open," all the girls reiterated several times. Recognition of my surroundings slowly began to return to me, although I didn't remember hitting my head at all. I tried to stand up, but when I walked the ground seemed to move up and down. My head was aching.

"We need to take you to the health center on campus," said my counselor.

"Oh, please don't tell my mom. Please don't call her," I pleaded as I walked with my counselor to the health center, where they performed some test on me and satisfied themselves that I was OK. From that day on I stayed close to the counselors who were in charge of escorting us to our college classes in the different buildings. The up-and-down wavy feeling persisted for a week, making it difficult to walk, but I was still grateful for the wonderful experience I was having. Nothing, not even a concussion, was going to rob me of my fun and the joy of being away from home.

However, I did begin to feel isolated and alone, much more than I ever had before. The food incident with my Reading teacher earlier that year had been a turning point in my life: I had consciously resolved to keep everything a secret. I felt changed by that one semester alone with Mom. I felt even more vulnerable around her now, and the event of the sudden seizure made me feel especially isolated and alone. The other girls wondered what could be wrong with me, and I too was puzzled. I knew the seizure was somehow connected with my abuse at home; perhaps my body just couldn't handle the sudden change in environment, the quick 180-degree shift from oppression and stress to freedom and release. Maybe it just freaked my body out. Mom was finally not around to bang my head against something, so I went off and got it banged anyway. Walking next to my counselor I remembered how before, when I'd had appendicitis, I had similarly begged my teachers not to send me home. I knew this kind of response created doubt in the minds of teachers and counselors, but I wasn't about to get myself sent home early from Paradise. I would just suck it up and deal with the concussion myself. Besides, getting my head badly banged wasn't anything I wasn't already used to dealing with at home.

Soon camp came to a close. I had become very close to my counselors and friends. I cried a lot the day we all said goodbye, and for many days afterwards.

10

Fireworks and Raisins

The Fourth of July was around the corner, and fireworks were one of my favorite things in life. Whenever I listened to the soundtrack of *The Sound of Music*, I always loved singing the song "My Favorite Things" and thinking of my own favorite things—one of which was definitely fireworks. My hometown always put on such a spectacular display, and I could always get a perfect view of it from our front yard. We had a concrete sidewalk that went up the center of our front lawn, to a set of steps ascending between the two towering retaining walls. I would sit on the sidewalk close to the bottom of the lawn, near the street where our brick mailbox was, and watch.

July Fourth came, and all day I looked forward to that night, cleaning extra hard and trying even harder than usual to please Mom so she would let me watch the fireworks.

Finally, the sky darkened; the time for the show was nearing. As I scurried around the house trying to complete the day's chores, I came flying around a corner and careened into my mother. She threw a fierce look at me. She knew that I was happy. I trembled under her gaze.

"You may not watch the fireworks tonight."

I dropped to my knees and let out a cry of agony. I had looked forward to this all year! It only came once a year!

"I'm not changing my mind. I absolutely forbid you to watch the fireworks tonight."

Why?? I thought, but I didn't dare ask. I rose tearfully to my feet as she gave me orders to finish cleaning in the kitchen. Simply unable to hold back, I sobbed as I wiped out the microwave and polished the stainless steel handle on the fridge door. Soon the family gathered outside; I heard the clang of the front door being slammed. Again I dropped to my knees, and a frenzy of frustration came over me; the taste of freedom earlier that summer had made this experience all the more wrenching. I began to feel a tightness in my chest, and was overcome by a wave of hysteria. Why had she done this to me for no apparent reason? Well, she was Mom; she didn't need a reason.

I couldn't bear the sound of the booming fireworks outside while I remained trapped in the house, so I ran to my dad's office, which was down a hallway and not far from the kitchen. Frantic, I crawled under one of the many desks in the room, picking the one closest to the wall, and wailed at the top of my lungs as I curled up into a ball. I didn't want to feel anything right now; I just wanted to drown out everything, especially the sound of the fireworks, with my loud groaning. For once I didn't have to worry about Mom hearing me cry—or anyone, for that matter. I cried with all my heart. How could my own mother be so heartless?

How could she hurt me this way for no reason? For her, there would always be a reason to cause me pain, to punish me: the reason was *me*. She couldn't stand me.

I stayed under the desk until my parents made me go to bed. The next day my eyes were swollen from crying. The dark circles had returned, and I remembered what the other girls at camp had said to me about my eyes.

I was usually sent to bed before ten, but my weariness and my eyes were not helped by the fact that I didn't like to waste the solitude and peace of night by sleeping. I liked having my mind all to myself without having to worry about what I had to do or clean, and would spend hours just lying in bed thinking. I would think about Jesus and pray, and I would imagine myself somewhere else—mostly with Ann, or with my aunt or grandparents. I always imagined myself being hugged. I would yawn and try to fight back the sleepiness I felt so I could enjoy the comfort of my thoughts.

We had to get up early in the mornings to do our chores; it was always Dad who woke me up, and usually the hot cereal was already cooking on the stove. Cold cereal, milk, and bread had been cut out of our diet and I could not recall ever eating meat in my home. I noticed that with each year our list of admissible foods grew shorter. We had hot cereal in abundance, however—a different kind for each morning. Cream of wheat (the extremely healthy kind), Seven Grain, oat bran, oatmeal, millet, and other variations of porridge were prepared with water, little or no milk, and no sugar: we were allowed a few raisins for a hint of sweetness. My portion was always meted out to me with a fourth- or half-cup measure. The raisins were the highlight of my day; it was a treat to have even a few for my cereal, maybe once a week.

After breakfast one day, Mom took a shower instead of a bath, which meant I didn't have to read to her. Gabriel and I waited until we heard the clang of the shower door.

"Okay! Now is our chance," I said. "We have to eat them now if we're going to do this today. Do you promise that you won't tell? I will not admit to eating a single raisin if you agree to deny it with me," I promised my brother solemnly.

"I will deny it to the death."

"Okay, but we have to be quick. She takes such short showers. You stand watch and I'll get the raisins for us."

"All right. Hurry!" urged Gabriel. I quickly scurried off to grab a few raisins—not too many, in case she noticed. She watched the food levels like a hawk.

"I'm back," I said, breathless from my foray. "What a treat! I'm so hungry." After savoring the choice morsels, we hastily brushed our teeth and ran back to our desks. I continued reading my school book.

"Estella, I got some new books for you. You must always be filling your mind with educational things." Mom surprised me; I hadn't heard her come in. I was never allowed to shut my bedroom door under any circumstances, even if I was changing. I knew that Mom insisted on always being able to keep a watchful eye on my brother and me, but she kept a particularly sharp eye on me.

"Thanks, Mom!" I gleefully took the box of books from her hands. Being cooped up in the house all day wasn't all bad when you had interesting books to read.

"I don't want you reading now, though. I have a list of chores I'd like for you to accomplish first." I looked at the long, detailed list of instructions she had typed out for cleaning everything from the kitchen to the bedroom.

"I want you to do the dusting in the dining room first."

"Okay." I pushed my yellow chair away from my bedroom desk and grabbed my supplies: a polishing cloth for dusting wood, another cloth for wiping with 409 Cleaner, and a paper towel—a used one—for Windex.

There was a beautiful china cabinet in the dining room, filled with lovely glass ornaments and decorative figurines. Most of the figurines had been purchased by me, with the money I earned babysitting, and given as gifts to my mother. Deep down I knew I was trying to buy her love: cleaning hadn't done it, obedience counted for very little in this household even though it was strictly upheld, excelling at every talent was a fail, and physical displays of affection were out of the question. I felt a deep pang of guilt as I thought of my father's kindness and the fact that I never bought anything for him. Every day, the only way I could show him love was to ask the same question: "How was your day at work?"

The cabinet was filled with glass shelves. The shelves and everything on them had to be perfectly cleaned. We still had outside help with the cleaning, but Mom liked to keep me busy. I stood in front of the china cabinet and began to carefully remove each figurine, wiping each one off with my half-used paper towel. Mom left me to go into the kitchen, but she was still only a short distance away; I watched nervously out of the corner of my eye as she opened the fridge.

"Who's been into the raisins?" she demanded.

"Not me."

"Not me," echoed my brother. I had backed away from the china cabinet.

"I know you've eaten some of the raisins," declared Mom, several times.

I shook my head.

"No, Mom, I haven't touched the raisins." I had resolved not to crack, no matter what. Mom cornered my brother and accused him of eating them too. Gabriel uttered a defiant no.

"I know that you are lying to me."

"Mom, all we've had is the oat bran you gave us for breakfast."

She quickly moved toward me and slapped me several times across the face. Then she grabbed me by the shoulder and began to drag me through the kitchen into a hallway that connected to the laundry room. It was a dark part of the house. She thrust me to the floor.

"I'll be back." She returned soon with my brother and thrust him into the dark, narrow hallway next to me. "Now admit to it, or I will punish both of you severely."

How bad could it be? I thought. After all, she couldn't possibly know with absolute certainty that we had eaten only a few raisins. She would have to punish us with at least a doubt in her own mind. I vehemently denied eating any raisins. Suddenly Mom sprinted off, came back with a board, and proceeded to whack both of us many times with it. We stalwartly continued to deny eating any of the raisins.

"You're driving me crazy!" she screamed, swiping at me with her fingernails.

Dad came home for lunch, and I knew that my face was still red from all the slapping and crying.

"They're driving me crazy. I know that food is always disappearing from the kitchen, and they always deny it, always!" declared Mom.

Dad gave us the "Don't Drive Mom Crazy" speech, and then Mom ordered us back to our cleaning jobs. I was beginning to think that sneaking food wasn't worth it, but that thought lasted only until the next hunger pang.

"I'm putting the raisins in a Tupperware container from now on," announced Mom. I watched as she carefully emptied the bag of raisins into the Tupperware, making very neat layers. The layers were perfect: even if just one raisin was missing, she would now be able to tell without a doubt. I knew that we would have to wait until next week before we could sneak any more food; it would be another interminable week of hunger.

A few days later when I was again hungry, I contemplated my strategy. *I absolutely have to get smarter at this sneaking food thing.*

"Gabriel, let's sneak the raisins again," I proposed. "I know a way. Besides, she would never suspect that we would risk it again so soon after last week." It was shower day again for Mom, and as soon as the water started running I quickly darted into the kitchen. After opening the bottom drawer of the fridge, I carefully removed one complete single layer of raisins, replaced the container, and gently closed the fridge door. I wiped away the slight traces of fingerprints I had left on the stainless steel door handle, and ran to my brother who was still standing watch. We gulped down the raisins, practically swallowing them all whole.

"I wish I had enjoyed them more," I commented afterwards. But that night, before bed, while we brushed our teeth side by side, we gave each other a triumphant look. Victory! Mom hadn't even noticed. She never guessed that we would be gutsy enough to eat an entire layer of raisins. It was hard to believe that we had been punished so severely for eating just a few, and had now gotten away with eating over ten each without raising any suspicions. However, I felt pangs of guilt as I thought of how I had deceived my mother.

11

A Day in the Life

I was in my closet investigating my dress-up clothes. I had always wanted a hoop skirt like Scarlet O'Hara from *Gone with the Wind*. Taking down several hangers, I first straightened them out and then connected them to make one big circle, over which I carefully draped my old-fashioned floor-length skirt. The hangers poked through the material.

"This is not what I envisioned," I said out loud, and gave up for the time being. Grabbing my book, I crawled underneath the clothes hanging from the closet rail, positioning myself so that I could see through the grating over the vent. The vent was supposed to improve the circulation of air through the house, but I appreciated it for another reason. Getting down on my knees to read, I looked through the grating to get a perfect view of the hallway into my parents' bedroom, knowing that they couldn't see me. I kept watch. Shutting my bedroom door was forbidden, and one of the hardest things for me to cope with was the surprise presence of Mom in my bedroom. I felt like I needed the extra few seconds' warning to brace myself for the impending attack. I would watch for the flash of Mom's spotless white sneakers and listen for any sounds of footsteps.

I became engrossed in the book I was reading. I had read all the Nancy Drew books and now I was into *Little House on the Prairie*; after *Little House on the Prairie* I would start on *Anne of Green Gables*. Then suddenly, in my peripheral vision, I caught a flicker of movement through the vent: Mom's footsteps were taking her out of the bathroom, and she was marching quickly. I flew to the floor by my bed and returned my gaze to the page full of words, but I had ceased to read. I knew what was coming. Mom burst through the half-open door to my bedroom.

"Get in here." I jumped up as I received several slaps across the face, too many to count. I was becoming sick with resentment at all the slapping.

I hate you. I hate you. I hate you, I thought. These were the only words I was aware of; I didn't hear anything my Mom was saying to me as she dragged me down the hall, my legs and knees scraping against the carpet. I tried to walk, but she pulled me down so hard and fast. We arrived in the master bedroom.

"Do you see the corner of the sheet that you left untucked beneath the comforter? You never follow directions! You are such a disobedient child. And did you see this?" She pointed to the remote lying on top of the TV. "You know that the remote goes in this special holder. How many times do I have to tell you to keep the remote in the holder at all times, *all times?*"

"I forgot, Mom."

"Don't make excuses, and just look at the bed."

"I thought I tucked it in, Mom."

"Stop defending yourself." She slapped me again and again, and I winced under the sting of her hot hand. I would be so embarrassed when Dad got home from work and would be asked to spank me again.

"I'm sorry, Estella. I should not have hit you like that." Her face softened inexplicably, and I relaxed. But then her glance went back to the TV remote, and the mere sight of it must have riled her up again, because she suddenly reverted to slapping me, letting up just long enough for me to replace the remote where it belonged. Trying to tune out her tirade and my pain, I thought of the last time I'd watched TV, and how I was never allowed to just sit down and watch it; Mom always forced me to stay frantically busy with tasks I could do while seated. She was the one who liked watching television. As if reading my evil thoughts, she dug her fingernails into my arm and hurled me into the dresser.

"You also missed a spot on the silk plant that you cleaned."

"I'll fix it right now." I turned toward the kitchen to fetch a rag and was walking away when she grabbed me from behind. I flinched with fear. She quickly lifted my shirt and clawed my back with her fingernails.

"Fix the bed!" she snarled. So I turned back around to fix the little flap of sheet that was just barely visible hanging out from under the comforter. As I lifted the corner of the mattress she barked at me again.

"Don't do it like that. Do it like this," she demanded.

"Oh, yeah, Gran showed me to do it that way," I said nervously, trying to be agreeable.

"No, she didn't. You think Gran taught you everything. *I* taught you everything. *I* taught you how to tuck a sheet in long before Gran did. Stop defending yourself." Another hot hand met my cheek on both sides.

I stood there wishing to God that I could just pass out. I didn't understand how my body could always hold up under all the slapping. I wanted so badly to fall to the ground in a dead sleep and never wake up. Why had I mentioned Gran, of all people? It had just popped out of my mouth. I watched as Mom tucked the sheet under the mattress to demonstrate.

"See? Now you do it." She jerked the sheet out all the way around the bed, and I stooped to lift the mattress again, every nerve in my body on edge as Mom stood with her body almost against mine. I shook and trembled, gripped by fear from head to toe, and flinched again as she raised her hand. *She was just reaching for the sheet, wasn't she? Why did I flinch?* I chastised myself.

"I told you to stop flinching! How come you keep flinching?" I knew that I wasn't supposed to answer that question. "Go clean the dining room. Every square inch of it!"

I left the master bedroom as Mom followed me into the dining room. She stood over me while I carefully dusted the already clean glass shelves. At least my used paper towel was indisputably shredded and I could get a fresh one. It was hard to clean the glass with used paper towels; Mom always complained about the little pieces of lint. After dusting, I reached up with the bottle of Windex and instantly felt a death grip on my tiny wrist.

"Don't spray the Windex in the cabinet. You might get spots on the wood. Spray the rag." I shot a few squirts of Windex onto the dry paper towel, and received another slap across the face. *I hate you*, I thought.

"I told you, only *one* squirt of Windex. You're wasting it. It's not your money you're wasting, it's ours! Besides, you might get blue spots on the white carpet." I felt bad for wasting Mom and Dad's money; after all, she spent so much money on books and homeschool curriculum for me. She paid for my ballet and piano lessons too, and the fun college camp I had been to last summer. I shivered. I felt cold, deeply cold. I always got cold when Mom was like this with me. I felt sweat begin to drip down the inside of my shirt from under my arms.

"I'm sorry, Mom." My mind drifted back to ballet. I had planned to get my first pair of pointe shoes for my birthday. Mom and Dad had taken me to be fitted for them and then, at the last moment, Mom had changed her mind. She said that I needed to be punished and that I had to wait; I didn't know for how long. My twelfth birthday had come and gone and I had not received the pointe shoes. I wondered now if I would ever get them.

"Now, wipe off the mini-blinds throughout the entire house with a damp cloth—*gently*," she commanded in a stern tone. I began cleaning the mini-blinds. They seemed so delicate. Mini-blinds were hard to clean because the dirt buildup on each little slat did not lift off easily. I meticulously cleaned each little strip of plastic, making sure my rag was barely damp lest excess water cause dirty rivulets to run all the way down the blinds, leaving ugly streaks.

Dad came home from work hours later. I had finished cleaning the dining room and Mom's precious mini-blinds, and now stood in the bathroom, hesitating to emerge. I closely inspected my face in the mirror: it was still red. I lifted up my shirt and craned my neck to see my back and arms. Claw marks were everywhere; I could see where the blood had risen to the surface. I returned to my room.

One more hour and I think my face will be clear, I thought as I slipped on a different shirt to hide the marks left by Mom's attack. I went back into the closet and hid underneath the clothes again. It was dark outside; the days were getting shorter. I shut the closet door and felt a slight relief being in the dark. I felt hidden, but I knew it was a false sense of security.

Oh, my gosh! I caught my breath. Mom was walking down the hallway. I would be in so much trouble if she caught me with the closet door shut. Silently turning the doorknob, I squeezed through the cracked-open door and quickly opened a dresser drawer, pretending to be rummaging through my clothes.

"Let me see you," Mom barked as she whipped me around by the shoulder. "All right, you can come out of your room now. It's time for you to cook dinner." I walked into the kitchen.

"How was work today?" I asked Dad, throwing him a fake smile as Mom passed me a handful of vegetables to prepare. I asked him the same question every day; I didn't know what else to say. Besides, I wasn't allowed to say much to Dad anyway.

"It was fine—" Dad began, and was instantly interrupted by Mom.

"Here. Spray the vegetables with this special spray first, then put soap on the scrubber and scrub them," she said. Mom had a special way of doing everything, but soap on vegetables seemed a little excessive. I said nothing and obeyed. Finally, when I had finished preparing the meal, I was able to sit down to eat at the counter for just a minute before Mom asked me to get up and do something else. I stared down at the little bit of bell pepper and few little pieces of broccoli on my plate, and ate it up quickly even though I didn't exactly feel hungry.

We watched an educational TV show that night and I was assigned all the socks to sew up. We had plenty of money;

Mom could easily buy new socks, but I knew she saved everyone's worn-out ones just to keep my hands busy. I looked at the pile of socks on the couch, each one with multiple holes, and was reminded of the story of Rumpelstiltskin from the Brothers Grimm (I had a two-volume collection of their fairy tales that I loved reading), about the girl who had to stay in a roomful of straw and spin it into gold for three nights in a row.

At the end of the day, weary from all that had happened, I was finally allowed to collapse into bed. I would not be doing any daydreaming tonight. I was too exhausted to think.

12

Stolen Candy

Weeks and then months passed. No one outside the family knew how Mom was treating me all the time. I dreaded each day, but always found hope in getting out of the house to babysit or go to church. I usually babysat once a week for two different families. I finally obtained my pointe shoes, after Mom saw that I had suffered sufficiently. I had fallen in love with ballet and practiced piano as often as possible. I was very involved in church on Wednesdays and Sundays, but I missed my friends; I rarely had a chance to hang out or visit with them anymore. But I loved seeing my favorite person every Wednesday and Sunday, and thrived on the hugs I received from people at church. Remembering them, and the time spent with Ann, is what helped sustain me through the long, dreary hours of wiping mini-blind after mini-blind, scrubbing baseboard after baseboard, and receiving slap upon slap from Mom's hot hands.

It was late in the evening and I was waiting to attend choir practice at church. I loved running around in the church when it was empty; I felt the same freedom in the empty church building that I experienced when I was allowed to ride my bike around the neighborhood. In the moments before the choir assembled and practice got underway, I was feeling hungry, and suddenly remembered that the Sunday School classroom was loaded with candy. *Easy-access food!* I thought, and ran down the long flights of steps to the familiar Sunday School room. I opened the cabinet door. *They won't mind if I take a piece,* I rationalized, quelling any inhibitions. I had grasped a treat and was closing the cabinet door when I looked up. In the doorway stood my mother. She flew at me in a controlled rage.

"Estella, how *dare* you!"

She flung me into the car and roared off toward home. As soon as we got into the house I raced inside, not daring to look back, ran to the bathroom, and flung open the door. I slammed it shut in absolute desperation, pressed the lock button, and held it down with my finger as I stood sandwiched between the toilet and the wall. The space was narrow. I could hear the clang of Dad's closet door in the background: Mom was getting the belt. Soon I felt the doorknob twist. I held the lock down fast. I knew Mom could not unlock the door from the outside as long as I held the button down with my finger.

"Estella, you open up this door right *now!*" she commanded in her most fearsome tone.

"No, Mom. I can't. You'll kill me." I was terrified beyond reason. I didn't want to be slapped and belted to death. I knew I was violating a direct command by being in the bathroom with the door locked, but Mom was going to kill me anyway, so it didn't matter.

"Estella, you open this door now! I am going to pulverize your little body!" threatened Mom, as if I needed reminding. My heart sank. I felt wedged in, like a board at the sawmill about to be cut in two. I knew there was no escape, but maybe I could put off my punishment until Dad came home. Mom continued to pound on the door with her fist. She was enraged, but she couldn't break down the door. I crouched on the hard floor, my finger growing numb from pushing down on the lock, and soundlessly changed fingers. I waited and waited and waited, weary with fear. Finally, Dad came home. After some coaxing, he convinced me to open the bathroom door to receive my punishment.

I didn't think I would live through that day, but I survived, and I never took candy or treats from the Sunday School classroom again.

Summer finally arrived, and I looked forward to multiple trips out of town to visit relatives, alone and away from Mom. I was allowed to rejoin the youth group to a certain extent, and went backpacking with them. I loved hiking in the mountains of New Mexico.

I also enjoyed helping take care of my baby cousin Abby when I visited my Aunt Jade. Little Abby was so much fun! I cried so hard when I had to leave her and my aunt. I also went to visit my grandparents and great-grandparents, and they let me eat ice cream and see a play. After that I traveled to Girl Scout Camp, where I had gone every summer since I was very young. This was my seventh year there, and by now I was best friends with the full-time staff. I had been trained to lifeguard at camp, and received special treatment this year in my position of responsibility. My friend had been to camp almost as many years as I had, so we stuck together like glue and helped out wherever we could. The counselors were especially friendly to us, and I felt relief from the year of terror I had endured with Mom. She seemed so much worse than before, and had actually installed bars on several windows around the house, on the outside. Our home was fast becoming more and more a jail and less and less a home. I couldn't believe she had still allowed me to go away for so much of the summer.

It was the best year of camp I had ever experienced. Two weeks after it was over, I was packed off to the Gifted and Talented college camp for my second year. Two weeks of dorm food was wonderful, but my favorite was the hot chocolate machine, and I began each day with a cup of hot cocoa. Mom would never know. My counselors this year were two best friends in their twenties who were exceptionally kind to me and French-braided my hair. During my stay that year, I finally convinced a girl my own age to teach me how to French-braid my own hair. It always seemed easier on other people.

"No, it's easier on yourself. It's hard to French-braid other people's hair," my friend promised.

"How can that be? I've been French-braiding other people's hair for a long time, but I've never been able to do my own. I always have to get other people to do it."

"Well, I'll show you how, and then you'll believe me." My friend guided me through the process, and I practiced and practiced.

"Wow!" I said when I'd finally mastered it. "You're right! It *is* easier on myself."

I met a boy my own age at camp—the director's son—and he asked me to the camp dance. Every girl in camp wanted to be chosen by him for the camp dance! I also got to know a lovely Chinese girl named Polly Dimke, and found out she lived in a suburb of Dallas named Cedar Hill, close to my grandparents. We became fast friends and did everything together. I hoped I would be able to see her in Dallas someday.

When camp ended, I cried a lot, especially at night. I would clutch my Cabbage Patch dolls close, reminding myself of how my counselors had hugged me at camp. I felt devastated by having to return home, but consoled myself by writing to my counselors, who diligently and kindly wrote back. I would read and reread their letters, keeping each one tucked away in a special drawer. Once in a while I occupied myself with journaling, taking great care never to write anything in my journal that Mom wouldn't like; I knew she could find and read my journal without warning. I was careful to write only about happy experiences, including mention of how attached I felt to my grandmother. I missed everyone I had visited in the summer. Gran had taken me ice skating and to a water park. Aunt Jade usually took us to Six Flags, or to Wet'n'Wild. It would be another year before I would get a chance to do those fun things again.

13

Nightmares and a Vision

I had turned thirteen years old and I was still being homeschooled. I was allowed to see my best friends Lauren and Madison once in a while, but not nearly as often as I wished. I made a lot of new friends in the homeschool group, and loved going to spend the night at their homes when I got the chance. I was so relieved to get away from my house that I was simply overjoyed each time I left it. I enjoyed the playtime best of all.

I was still very involved at church, singing, playing the piano for offertory, and ringing handbells. I also attended youth group, where I would sometimes sneak a soda. I only ever drank Sprite. I had never tasted any other soda, but I called all the different kinds "Coke"; if it was carbonated, then it was "Coke" to me. Mom always watched my plate carefully during our church dinners to make sure I didn't serve myself portions that were too great, but after church dinner I was excused to youth group while Mom stayed downstairs to listen to the pastor's sermon. I guess I got careless or foolhardy from all the times I had gotten away with sneaking a soda, because this time I sat drinking my Sprite when suddenly I felt the familiar iron grip on my arm, and looked up in horror at my mother standing over me. She had come up from the sermon and the look of fire was in her eyes. She motioned for me to back quietly out of the meeting, and let go of my arm, but ordered me to march to the car: we were leaving immediately.

Once we got home, I received the usual slaps and spankings. She made Dad spank me too. I hated that the most. By then Dad was spanking me more than ever at Mom's every whim, always on the bare backside. It filled me with shame. *I would have been spanked for something anyway, even if she hadn't caught me with the Sprite,* I thought to myself. However, that was the end of youth group.

I later learned from my youth pastor that he and his wife, noticing my skinniness, had called a meeting with my parents. My mom had told them that she knew I was anorexic and that she was taking me to a psychiatrist about it. This was a lie. My parents then recommended they not tell anyone, to avoid embarrassing me. No doubt the pastor's suspicion was the real reason I was pulled from youth group.

No one suspected what it was really like for me at home, and I never entertained the thought of telling anyone. I felt humiliated and embarrassed just thinking about my life with Mom and Dad. Every time we took a family trip, the first thing Mom and Dad would do upon arrival at our destination (usually a museum) was take me into the public bathroom and spank me; Dad would even come into the women's bathroom to spank me at Mom's command.

The worst part about leaving town with Mom and Dad, though, was the actual trip. I would usually need to use the restroom along the way, and Mom would always follow me into the bathroom and stand over me. I would get so nervous I wouldn't be able to go, and this would frustrate her to no end. She would slap me while I was sitting down, trying to go, and I would usually get back into the car having accomplished nothing except getting into more trouble.

So I was glad when the trips out of town to various museums were over. We had returned home from Dallas, and it was almost my birthday. My relatives always sent the best gifts. I lay in bed thinking how strange life was. There were good points about being out of town. For one thing, I felt safer once we were with relatives. But on the other hand, Mom still hit me in their back guest rooms, and then I would be afraid to come out. I loved being with my relatives and being out of town, but I hated the car trips.

That night I dreamed I went to the bathroom in the middle of the hallway, on the white carpet. I woke up with a start.

It was already bright outside. Why hadn't Dad woken me up? *What a nightmare,* I thought, remembering what I had dreamed. *Mom's white carpet is her pride and joy.* I slipped the special tennis shoes on that were for use only in the house because of the white carpet, and walked out of my bedroom, through my bathroom doorway, into the hall. I stopped in shock, hardly able to believe my eyes, and blinked. Surely my eyes were playing tricks on me! I opened my eyes again, and there was no question: there in the middle of the white-carpeted hallway was a large yellow stain. *Oh, my gosh. That was no nightmare. That was real.* I looked up. Why hadn't Dad or Mom woken me up this morning? They must not have seen the spot; maybe they had passed through the hallway while it was too dark to see. I looked down at the spot again in disbelief, and when I lifted my eyes again I saw Dad pass through the little brown doors. His gaze met mine. I could tell by the look in his eyes that he had just noticed the large stain on the white carpet. Suddenly, Mom came up behind him.

"I did that," I said, pointing, "in my sleep. I was dreaming, only I guess that part wasn't really a dream." Mom and Dad just looked at each other and said nothing, so I turned and walked back into my bedroom. The stain was so large, and Mom so particular about her carpet, I knew she would want to try and remove the discoloration herself. I could not imagine what Mom and Dad would do to me. I was traumatized at the thought of having done this when all the while I thought I was dreaming. *Something must be really wrong with me, seriously wrong with me, to have done something like this in my sleep,* I reasoned. Later that day Mom and Dad came to me.

"We believe this has happened to you because your dolls are evil, so we're throwing all of your Cabbage Patch dolls away. Okay?"

"Okay. I understand," I said, still in shock and not fully registering what they had said. I did not want this accident ever to happen again, no matter what the cost. Mom and Dad began removing all my Cabbage Patch dolls and related paraphernalia, things I had been collecting for years. That night as I peered through the bay window, I saw the dumpster piled high with all of my toys, and realized I would never see them again.

I liked summers, but it was good to be back into the school year, too. I resumed my ballet and piano and babysitting. I had been babysitting for the same two families for four years now. They also went to my church, so I got to see the

kids on Sundays as well as during the week. I liked hanging out in the church nursery and volunteering my time. I felt as if the kids were practically related to me, as if I had the little brothers and sisters I had always dreamed of.

If I completed my chores for the day, I was often allowed to go outside and ride my bike, as long as it was after four in the afternoon; any earlier than that, and Mom was afraid the sun would hurt my skin. Gabriel and I loved riding our bikes the most, but we also enjoyed the pogo stick and skates we had received on our shared birthday. I remained heavily involved in drama at church, besides all the music I was involved with. Piano had exploded in my life; it was my primary outlet at home, as practicing was something Mom would nearly always allow me to do. Sometimes, though, if I played too much or too loud, she would come bursting into the room through the double doors, throwing them open with such force that the doorknobs would strike the walls. The defeaning sound always made me jump, was my cue to take a break. I marveled at how accomplished I had become on the piano, enough to enjoy playing almost anything I heard on my classical CDs. I loved listening to them while I cleaned and while I slept at night. It helped to calm my anxiety, especially while I slept. I *can't believe I stuck with piano,* I thought to myself as I remembered all the early years of merciless lessons given by Mom. I remembered how she had slapped me through each lesson, with zero tolerance for mistakes. I was so glad I had finally passed Mom and she had started me with the teacher across the street.

One day as I was sitting at the piano, I looked up through the tall windows into the courtyard. *I'd better go prune the roses,* I thought, and walked outside. Noticing my favorite cat, Cubby, rubbing up against my leg, I paused in my work to pick her up.

"You are my miracle kitten after I lost Sunshine," I told her, looking into her eyes. I had found her when she was just a very small kitten, years before, when I was much younger. After we'd had her for several years, Mom had informed me that we couldn't afford to keep her any more, and had driven Cubby and her two little baby kittens to a distant neighborhood and dropped them off. I had cried so much at having to say goodbye to my beloved cat. Then one day I had looked up from the kitchen into the courtyard, and there she stood! I hardly recognized her because she was so thin; it had been two weeks since Mom had dropped her off, and Cubby looked like she hadn't eaten in all that time. After she returned, Mom and Dad didn't have the heart to send her away again. Cubby was starting to seem old to me now after all she had experienced: she had been bitten by a rattlesnake, and lived through that too.

"You are my miracle kitty," I repeated, stroking Cubby's soft black coat. I went back to pruning the rosebushes in the courtyard, cutting off each faded bloom; it was my job to keep them looking nice, and it was one task I didn't mind. The roses were pretty, and when Mom wouldn't let me go anywhere, I found solace in being close to them. They reminded me of life, and their brilliant colors seemed to foster hope inside my heart. God had made each rose so beautiful! When would he make my life beautiful, I wondered, looking down at my body. Mom had told me that I was fat. *That's why I'm not allowed to eat much,* I thought as I carefully pruned off each dead bud.

I snuck food on a regular basis now. Gabriel and I had improved our technique for sneaking food and were more successful, but I still went to bed hungry almost every night. I went to sleep that night imagining myself at church. I was with Ann, and she was hugging me and telling me that she loved me. Then all of a sudden my eyes jerked open. Mom was dragging me out of bed. I felt a slap across my face. I couldn't see much because it was still so dark in my bedroom, and my arms flailed about as my body fell onto our white carpet with a thump.

"You left the dish brush in the sink. Get in there," railed Mom, pushing me half-awake into the hallway, through the brown doors into the living room, and then into the kitchen.

"I'll move it, Mom."

"Then you will rewrap the cord on the vacuum, because you did a bad job earlier."

Additional slaps met my already stinging cheeks. *I hate you. I hate you. I hate you,* I thought over and over again with each slap.

I was finally allowed to return to bed. But I never wanted to sleep again. I wanted to stay alert and not be startled by Mom. *I wish I could sleep with the door closed so that I could at least hear her when she busts in at night, I told Jesus with a sigh.* I tried to stay awake, but drowsiness got the best of me.

Gabriel and I worked very hard during the day, both at homeschooling and cleaning. This morning Dad had woken me up and Mom had given instruction about the mini-blinds. Several windows, all much larger than myself, made up most of each wall surrounding the courtyard. The game room had three windows, the living room six, and Mom's bedroom three more. Each window had glass-encased mini-blinds that could be turned by a small knob at the bottom. These mini-blinds, unlike the others in the house, never needed to be cleaned, because they were enclosed between the panes of glass and hence protected from dirt and dust. All we had to do was keep the glass sparkling clean. I stood in the living room as my Mom gave new instructions.

"In the morning the mini-blinds in the living room need to be cranked at a forty-five-degree angle in order to allow the morning sun in. This will heat up the living room in the winter. The game room mini-blinds need to be opened to a horizontal position before I begin my workout, to let in the rising sun. My bedroom mini-blinds must, at the same time, be tilted slightly to let in the morning light. At 10:00, as the sun moves, you must go around the entire house and change the angle of all the mini-blinds. The bedroom blinds then need to be opened completely horizontally to allow the full light of day, while the game room will be receiving direct sunlight and therefore needs to have its mini-blinds tilted up. This will allow some light, but direct light will be reflected upward. The living room mini-blinds will need to be adjusted also. You must see that no direct sunlight hits the furniture in the living room or it will bleach it out, but we do need to let some sunlight in so as to save on our heating bill. You need to stay on top of this all-day task morning, mid-morning, noon, and afternoon. In the evening all mini-blinds need to be fully closed."

I felt overwhelmed.

"Yes, Ma'am," Gabriel and I replied. We scurried around, each taking different rooms and taking care to follow her instructions. I was cold. Mom kept the thermostat set at fifty-two degrees in the winter, but running around all day helped me stay warm.

"Estella," Mom called. I ran to her side.

"I want you right here next to me doing what I tell you. Why were you way over on the other side of the house?"

"I was fixing the mini-blinds," I explained reflexively, flinching as I realized I had just defended myself. Defending myself was a no-no. Sure enough, a smart slap landed on my face. *I hate you,* I thought, without meaning to. It had become a habit.

"Don't defend yourself. I've told you that a hundred times."

I followed Mom around the house until after lunch. That afternoon I sat on the carpet in my bedroom with my head resting against the yellow dust ruffle around my twin bed. My bed was made; I was never allowed to sit on my bed when it was made, and it was always made. Mom was always afraid that I would damage the comforter if I sat on my bed. I was thinking about how often I thought the words "I hate you." I felt bad for hating my own mom. I didn't want to hate her anymore, and believed with all my heart that God did not like it either.

"I know what I will do from now on," I thought out loud. "I will think *I love you* every time she hits me." It was as if God had put the thought into my mind. I knew that even if I felt hate in my heart, changing my thoughts was bound to help me to feel more love for Mom eventually.

That night I wrote in my journal.

November 14

Last weekend I went to a slumber party at my friend's house. We camped outside in a big tent and roasted marshmallows, and I got to ride a mule. I had a blast! I was glad they lived in the country. This weekend I spent the night with my best friend till Saturday at 9:15 a.m. I was sad later because I couldn't go to the Symphony with Ann because I had gone to spend the night at my best friend's house. But there's always next time. I hope!

Enough with being sad. I'm going to be in a mime in the Sunday morning service to the song called "Thank You." I have a very good part. The adult bell choir is ringing bells this Sunday and Ann's first grade choir class is singing also.

My mom seems to be doing better. She's been drinking the super concentrated hydrogen peroxide and it seems to be helping a lot. I'm having a little problem with my wrist called carpal tunnel syndrome. I have faith it will go away and not get too serious. I so want to excel in ballet, but I know I must not rush my dancing. Oh! And by the way, Journal, if I read you when I'm old and gray, know that I learned my good cooking from my own professional cook—Mom! She has a degree in Hotel Restaurant Institutional Management.

Nothing has happened to Dad so far. I know that I can't imagine the fullness of the pain that his departure might cause. Will he go to heaven soon? If he dies, even in my lifetime, I think I can handle it.

I stopped writing. My hands were tired from the day's work. I thought of how Mom and Dad had told us that Dad was going to die. They didn't know how or when, but Dad was going to die. I didn't get to talk to Dad much; Mom didn't allow it. I had to always stay focused on chores and keep busy with schoolwork. So I couldn't speak to him about this even though it weighed on my mind.

I set my journal aside, half-hiding it among a lot of other books, and sighed. I hoped Mom would never see it, but if she did, I had taken precautions by what I had written and not written. Now it was time to go to bed. I had given up on ever hugging Mom good night; for years I had tried to hug her good night, but she never responded. She would just continue sitting at her desk, doing whatever she was doing. Dad would usually go over Bible verses with us at night, though, just before bed. That evening he read a Bible verse out loud: "Children, obey your parents in the Lord, for this is right."

Gabriel read his Bible verse of choice: "It is better to dwell in a corner of a housetop than in a house shared with a contentious woman. Proverbs 25:24." And "A continual dripping on a very rainy day and a contentious woman are alike. Proverbs 27:15." I stared at my brother in wide-eyed amazement. I knew he had chosen these verses because Mom always argued at Dad. How could he be so brazen? Dad said nothing.

Then I shared my Scripture verse. Speaking of Jesus and God at the creation of the world, I quoted, "Then I (Jesus) was beside Him (the Father) as a master craftsman; and I was daily His delight, rejoicing in His inhabited world, and my delight was with the sons of men. Proverbs 8:30."

We said good night and I curled up in bed. My Scripture verse for that night reminded me of the very special encounter I had recently had with God. I closed my eyes, remembering, and could still see God standing there. I had been sitting on the carpet in my bedroom, reading my Bible and praying, and just quietly soaking up the precious presence of God, when suddenly I had been surprised by a vision. I saw myself on one side of the room and my Dad and Jesus on the other side. I saw my Dad step out toward me, when suddenly God put out his hand to stop him, saying, "No, she is mine."

As I remembered this, my eyes jerked open in amazement. I believed! I believed that I belonged to God my Father. God would be a Father to me always! I jumped out of bed to open my Bible and, amazingly, my eyes instantly fell on Job 31:18. "For, like a father, God has brought me up, caring for me since ever I was born." God's comforting words seemed to wrap me in their warmth.

"You are my Father, Lord. I trust you," I whispered quietly under my covers as I drifted off to sleep.

14

Christmas and a New Year

That year for Christmas we traveled out of town to visit my Great-Grammie. My aunt and cousins on my mom's side of the family were going to be there also, and I was excited to see them. The house was filled with the smell of baking when we arrived, and as soon as we walked in, Great-Grammie showed me the fresh hot biscuits in the oven. She had sandwiched butter between the flaky layers of each biscuit. The kitchen counter was filled with goodies. Gabriel and I weren't allowed to eat those things, but Great-Grammie always helped sneak food to us. She liked giving us jelly beans and chocolate.

When Mom left the room to use the restroom, I hastily swiped a packaged cinnamon roll, planning to eat it at night when Mom was busy visiting. Running to the linen closet, I carefully pulled a stack of sheets and linens away from the back of the narrow closet wall, leaving a space behind them into which I dropped the cinnamon roll. I made it back to the living room just in time, where I played with my baby cousin and played games with my aunt. Mom never played with us.

I looked up to see Mom motioning me to come with her. I stood up and followed her to the quiet, empty bathroom just past Great-Grammie's master bedroom, Mom grabbing me by the arm as soon as we were out of sight. Once we had rounded the corner she thrust me down and began hitting and slapping me. Silently, I tried to shield my face by lifting my arm, but that only made it worse: Mom hissed at me, outraged at my self-defense as her hand struck my bony outstretched limb. Her penetrating glare frightened me, and I knew that she was furious at me for trying to shield myself. She would inform Dad and twist it around, telling him that I had hurt her.

I started to cry at the thought of all the other family in the next room; now I wouldn't get to be with them for a while, as it would take my face a long time to lose its redness. Eventually Mom turned without a word and left me crouching there. I cried, not because she hit me but because I was afraid someone might have heard. If I came out too soon, then all my relatives would know that I had just been punished. For the next two nights Gabriel got to stay at Great-Grammie's house with everyone else, while Mom punished me by making me sleep with her at the hotel. I thought of all the wonderful food my brother was probably eating.

Finally, Christmas day came. I reveled in all the pretty things my relatives had given me. Great-Grammie had bought me a beautiful pink nightgown with a matching robe, and a new coat. Some of the gifts I received I knew

I wouldn't be allowed to keep; years before, whenever my other aunt had bought me gifts, they had been sold and Mom had pocketed the money. Other gifts would be added to our re-gifting collection, to be used as presents for my friends when their birthdays rolled around. The coat Great-Grammie bought me was lovely, but I knew that because it was new, Mom probably wouldn't let me wear it once we got home, except to church. Most of my clothes came from Mom's high school days, or from our neighbors down the street; the clothes they handed down to me were beautiful, but that was ended now that they had moved away. Although my grandparents always took me shopping, I had never been shopping with Mom except once, and that was only for a new dance outfit.

After Christmas Day it snowed, and we had a lot of fun making snowmen. It rarely snowed in my home town, so this was quite a wonderful treat for me. When Christmas was over, it was hard to say goodbye; not only had I so enjoyed being with my relatives, but I always felt a little safer when I was around all of them. On our first night back home, on December 30, I wrote in my journal.

Dear Journal,

Well, I had a great Christmas this year. We took our first trip in the new Suburban to Amarillo for Christmas, and stayed in the Five Seasons Inn this time instead of at Great-Grammie's house because several of my cousins were staying there. Aunt Jade, Uncle Jay, and Abby drove into Amarillo and stayed at Great-Grammie's house too, so there was no room for us. The inn had an indoor pool and great breakfasts. Gabriel got to stay at Great-Grammie's for two nights, though. We left on a Saturday night and went to Sunday School the next morning. It was hard for all of us to leave Abby. I better go now; I am having Madison spend the night tonight, so I had better get to work.

Love, Estella

I wrote more entries on New Year's Day and the following week, always careful to include only the most innocent content.

Age 13: Christmas with Great-Grammie.

Dear Journal,

Well it's the start of a new year. It's icy outside and the family are all sitting around the kitchen table. The fog outside is thick. I hope it will go away. I don't like it when the sun doesn't shine. Madison and I had fun at my house despite the fact that we didn't have much time to play—she had to leave at 8 a.m. and we slept in till 7:45. She spent the night earlier this week and we played backgammon and my new game of Bibleopoly. I forgot to show her the wooden go-cart that Dad made for Gabriel. Gabriel spray-painted it silver and forgot to put a tarp under the go-cart, so he got in trouble for spray-painting the courtyard silver. My goal this year is to excel in ballet and piano and to be in the Nutcracker Ballet in San Antonio. I'm trusting God to get into the ballet in San Antonio, which is five hours away from home. Well, that's all.

Estella

January 4

I have dance today at 6:00. I'm going to start memorizing the names of all the exercises we do in ballet so that when I try out for the Nutcracker in San Antonio I will be ready to do the dance steps to their proper names. Piano is coming along really well. My piano teacher said that I could play for the judge in the Guild Auditions this year, so I am working really hard on it. Piano always gives me a sense of peace. Sometimes it even settles a sour stomach.

We have really been working hard lately, cleaning the house. I need to play with Stefanie more often. She is a friend from down the street who is in my dance class. I don't have a boyfriend yet. I love babysitting the two little girls down the street, Audrey and Katelynn. We haven't gotten out of the homeschooling group, but we haven't been going to any of the Tuesday activities because it's too much trouble, since I babysit every Tuesday. I would rather babysit than go to homeschool activities. Besides, I sometimes see my homeschool friends on Fridays anyway.

Mom is sleeping better and her muscle disorder is doing better. We start school again today; Christmas went by so fast! I'm glad that I'm starting up my regular schedule of dance, bell choir, and piano. I just got in trouble for eating candy cane over the white carpet.

January 6

Dear Journal,

I babysat the three little boys that also live down the street from me. I took them outside while the baby finished taking his nap. After he woke up, I bundled him up and we all went outside again. Mom said that I looked brighter, happier, unburdened, and prettier today. I felt happy and good. Lately I've been trying to please Mom and—I say!—I'm doing a fine job. Dad is still here.

I have bell choir, dinner, and church today! I got taken out of Drama in December because I got in trouble for lying about how Gabriel and I were running through the house. But when January came, I decided to stay out of Drama because of the way the kids act. Mom and I don't feel right about me going to youth group either. School is going well.

Love, Estella

15

On Our Own at the Ranch

Gabriel and I were going to the Ranch without Mom, and I was so excited! Since Mom wasn't going along, maybe Gabriel and I would get to eat more. Since I wasn't allowed to eat much at home, I would usually take the opportunity to feed myself in the homes where I babysat, munching on whatever I could find in the pantry. I couldn't tell anyone I hadn't eaten dinner, as the parents would wonder about that. But Dad was different when Mom wasn't around, and would stop at the special ice cream place on the way down to the Ranch. I was filled with anticipation; I lived every day for the chance to be away. My goal was always to manage to hold on until the next time I would be let out of the house. Time seemed to stretch on and on while I waited for freedom.

Gabriel and I climbed into our family's new Suburban,

and I settled myself to read my latest book. I absolutely loved slipping away from this world into the world of whatever book I was reading. After reading for a while, I kneaded Dad's neck while he drove; I had strong hands from playing the piano for so many years, and liked to relieve the tension of driving for him. When we stopped at the ice cream place, it was sheer bliss to lick the luscious creamy vanilla from my cone as melted drops landed on my wrist. A short time later, the drive was over and we were walking into the Ranch house.

"Whoa. It is a mess in here," I commented to my brother.

"I'll say. Who did this? Whoever was here last did not clean up."

I scurried around with the dishcloth, wiping the table and countertop, and started tossing empty food cans into the trash. Before long the place was tidy, and Gabriel and I burst out the back door into the wild blue yonder.

"Look at this, Gabriel!" We both stared at a very old bike leaning against a wall.

"Wow. I bet this was Mom's when she was a kid," he replied, looking it over.

"Let's take it!"

"You don't think we'll get into trouble?" Gabriel said nervously.

"No way. Granddad won't care. This is his place. What's on it is his too, and he won't care."

"But it doesn't have any tires. Not really, anyway." Gabriel looked skeptically at the thin rubber-covered metal wheels.

"It will be rough, but it'll be better than having to walk everywhere."

We both hopped on, but the old bicycle didn't want to budge.

"Okay. You stay on, and I'll run and push you down the hill, and then jump on too," I said, with more confidence than the situation warranted. After much more effort than anticipated, we finally made it down the dirt road to the dam. The musty smell of mossy growth on all the trees filled the air, and I could hear the trickling of nearby streams and the louder, stronger rush of water flowing over the dam wall.

"Come on. Let's walk across the dam wall to the other side." Gabriel and I always liked to cross the thin beam of concrete that stretched to the other side of dry land. A matter of minutes brought us to the most dangerous part, where the water flowed over the lip of the wall.

"Hey, look at all the dead tree limbs that are trapped here," said Gabriel.

"Wow!" I peered down into the murky darkness. We were never allowed to swim in the water on the deep side of the dam wall because of water moccasin—poisonous water snakes—but we could swim almost anywhere else that we could find a hole. Gabriel reached down to pick up a stick from the water. His hands had barely grasped it when suddenly it moved. He jerked his hand back.

"Oh, my gosh! That was a snake!"

"Probably a water moccasin, if it was black. I wish I'd seen it! I was looking over there." I pointed, and we continued over to the other side, from whence we made our way back again by skipping across the creek beds. We stepped carefully from rock to rock, trying to avoid getting our feet wet; it was a game we always played. Besides, there were leeches in the water. I had actually seen one once! The very thought of a leech sucking our blood was revolting.

"Look, Gabriel. Another snake!" This one was small and close to the rocky bank. I swished water until the snake was forced close to land, and then crushed it with a rock.

I always thought wildlife was interesting, but poisonous snakes were just dangerous; every snake we killed made me feel that much safer. Afterward we made our way, with a lot of pushing and shoving, back to the Ranch house on the rickety bike we had found.

We could never do this sort of thing back home. At the Ranch we could wander almost anywhere we wanted, and I loved the freedom of just getting to play all day. That night we had homemade pizza for dinner and went to bed early. Gabriel and I had planned something special for the early morning hours of the next day.

Around 4:30 a.m. I was awakened by the usual sounds of wildlife that surrounded us at the Ranch.

"Come on, Gabriel. Wake up." Quickly, he emerged from under his covers and we both quietly slipped into our clothes. We didn't want to wake up Dad this early in the morning. Although we were mostly allowed to come and go as we pleased at the Ranch, taking off at this time of night would have met with disapproval. We bundled up in Granddad's warm clothes and walked carefully along the side of the next room that led into the kitchen. The Ranch house was very old, and the floors always creaked; after minutes of tiptoeing and praying that we wouldn't get caught, we made it successfully into the kitchen. I shoved a great big iron skillet inside the gigantic coat I was wearing as I motioned to my brother to grab a spatula and paper plates. I added frozen bacon, and Gabriel carried pancake mix and sausages. I shoved butter and maple syrup into my pockets.

This is brilliant, I thought. We crept out of the house through the kitchen door. Once we were a safe distance from the house, we began to talk. The crisp, cool air was moist and thick with the musty smell of moss. It felt good to be outdoors.

"The hunter's cabin is the perfect spot—and just look at all this fog! It'll perfectly mask the smoke. I'll make a log cabin fire," I said. Having been in Girl Scouts for years, I had learned how to build the perfect fire.

"I have the matches. I'm going to collect some kindling."

"Wait for me. I don't want to be here alone!" We scurried around, looking for suitable firewood. Soon, after arranging the kindling in the shape of a log cabin, I had a roaring fire going. I threw a large melt grate over it and put the frying pan on top.

"That smells so good," murmured Gabriel as pancake batter sizzled in butter. The butter turned brown and I flipped the pancakes. "Let's throw on some bacon now, too."

"All right. You know, Gabriel, I just love the early morning, the smell of this food cooking on top of the smell of the burning sticks, and the sizzling sound mixed with the snapping and crackling of the fire. This will be a wonderful breakfast!"

"You're not afraid of getting caught? You don't think we will be caught, do you?"

"Of course not. You know Dad never really worries about us out here. By the time he notices we're gone, he'll think we just left to walk down to the dam like we do every day."

"What about the smoke?"

"It's dark. He can't see it with all this fog. Let's enjoy our breakfast. Where do you think we should explore today?"

"How about the path off the road to Windgate's place?"

"Yeah, we rarely walk up in there. That would be fun. We should hike over the ridge. As long as we stay away from where the hog traps are, we should be good... The food's ready. Where are the plates?" Gabriel reached over and handed me a paper plate. When I had served up the hot breakfast, we wolfed it down like street urchins.

"This is so excellent! Yummmm." Gabriel pressed his sticky lips together.

"I can't believe it. I'm actually starting to get full."

"Well, we can't leave leftovers. The animals will get into it, and hunters or Dad might see it."

"I'm eating. I'm eating! Oh, my gosh. This is so wonderful! I forgot how delicious bacon tastes. Great-Grammie used to cook bacon for us. Remember?"

"Yeah, I remember. I don't think we'll get to see her much now; Mom probably won't let us go stay with her any more. We're getting too old. Besides, I heard Great-Grammie and Mom talking. Mom knows she is suspicious now. It's too risky for Mom to let us be around her."

"Well, Mom has always been so careless around Great-Grammie. I mean, last time we were there, Mom hit me right in the next room, Great-Grammie's own bedroom, in fact. Mom's not really scared of Great-Grammie, but I think you're right: she knows it's risky. Besides, Mom knows how much we like going. That alone is reason enough for her to keep us from visiting Great-Grammie's house."

"Yeah. Really! Oh, boy, I am so stuffed."

"Me too. Time to dowse the fire. Come on, let's go fetch water from the dam."

Soon we had dumped enough water on our little makeshift restaurant to sink a small ship.

"Look at that, Gabriel," I declared in awe, looking around. "The fog is starting to lift, and the smoke is just now gone from our fire. God's timing couldn't be more perfect!" Then, pointing to the old iron skillet: "Is it already cooled off?"

"Yep. Here, you can take it." I quickly shoved the skillet back into my outer pants, under the great overcoat I was wearing. We always layered up with clothing if we were going hiking in the early morning, because it was cold.

Before long we were slipping back into the Ranch house. I didn't even hear Dad, and guessed that he was still sleeping in the back of the house. I noiselessly slipped the iron skillet back into the cupboard, and Gabriel carefully buried the pancake mix in the bottom of the deep freeze where most of the food was stored. I felt so satisfied; I was ready to get down to some real fun now. I waved for the door, and soon Gabriel and I were running up the road to the creek bed. We slid down the muddy canyon walls lined with clayey rock and red dirt until we reached our favorite spot to begin our hike. It was a long way to the far-off spot we had chosen to explore today, but that was exactly why we had chosen it. We hiked for hours. I kept thinking that soon we would have to arrive at the top of the ridge.

"Come on. Just a little further," I kept repeating.

"I'm tired, Estella, and we're far from the house. Let's turn around." My brother always seemed more level-headed and reserved than me: I was impulsive and daring.

"All right. Let's turn around," I agreed reluctantly. We traipsed through more brush for what seemed like hours, slowly making our way back toward the dirt road we had left earlier. Finally I could make out the rocky canyon below, but we still had a long, steep walk to make it to the bottom of the hill. Turning my head to look back at my brother a short distance behind me, I took a step forward for balance, when suddenly the ground gave way underneath my feet. The few rocks I was standing on rolled down the steep cliff, and I fell and rolled about twenty-five feet down the slippery slope, feeling the soft, wet earth beneath my uselessly grasping hands. Stretching out my foot, I suddenly slammed up against a firm support and looked up behind me. My body had carved a smooth trail; mounds of loose leaves were piled up on either side of it, and all around me.

"Estella! Are you okay?" yelled Gabriel at the top of his lungs.

"Oh, my gosh! That was *so* much fun! Wow! You have to try it. I'm going to climb up and see if I can do that again."

"Are you crazy, Estella?"

"It's perfectly safe. The leaves will cushion your fall as you slide down. It's like a slide made of soft earth and leaves, millions of leaves," I explained, animated. Every year we managed to find new activities to keep our time at the Ranch exciting, but this was the best yet.

"Nothing will ever be able to top this," I said decidedly after another slide down the mountainside, as I called it. We took turns sliding down until the ground was literally bare. Mounds of leaves were now piled up at the foot of our makeshift slide; we tried gathering them up and covering the trail over again for sustained sliding. After hours of fun, we startled at the sound of a gunshot.

"Well, it's time to head back; that's our signal. Dad must be ready for us to come in." Gabriel and I marched wearily back to the Ranch house, where I washed off outside and then began to work on getting dinner ready: Velveeta shells and cheese.

What a wonderful day! I smiled to myself as I thought of the rich creamy cheese we were about to enjoy. Dad was much more laid back about what we ate. I fell into bed that night after a round of Monopoly in which Dad slaughtered us once again. *Couldn't he ever let us win?* I thought. I just was not good at amassing hotels and money. My eyes closed and soon I had drifted off to sleep. I never wanted this time to end.

The next day met us with a new discovery while we were searching Granddad's shed for supplies.

"What's this black stuff?" I asked.

"I don't know. It looks like some sort of powder."

"Oh, boy. It will be just like on Gunsmoke."

"Gunsmoke? What are you talking about? Gunsmoke is a TV show."

"I know, that old black and white show Mom is always watching. It is so boring, but I love the parts where they spread the black powder stuff along the floor and then light it at one end like a fuse. I love watching the spark race along the trail of powder."

"Are you crazy? Have you gone out of your mind?"

I was already halfway down the dirt driveway with the bag of powder.

"Come on!" I yelled, tossing my curly hair back. "I've got the stuff!" I had already slung the large, heavy bag over my shoulder and was hauling it to the dam wall. "We have to do this close to the water—on top of it, even!"

"Do what?"

"You'll see. Come on." Gabriel trailed behind me as we marched down to our usual spot at the dam. I struggled under the hot sun. Even in winter it still got hot, especially when you were carrying something heavy, like I was, and the sun was beating down. I carefully opened the bag of black stuff and lined the top of the dam wall with it. *Curious,* I thought, pressing the dry powder between my fingers. At the end of the black line of powder I placed a Styrofoam cup that I had been carrying in my pocket. I filled it up with more of the black powder.

"That's for the big boom at the end," I said. Gabriel's eyes opened about as wide as the mouth of the cup I had just filled up. I carefully struck a match and held it close to the thin line at the start of my long black trail, flanked by water on either side, and as it caught fire Gabriel trembled with awe.

"It's just like Gunsmoke," I said wonderingly. The fire followed the trail of black powder until it reached the cup, erupting in a grand finale with a good three-foot flame at the end.

"Wow!" Gabriel said. "I can't believe that worked!"

"We'd better not press our luck. Let's take it back now." I slung the heavy bag of gunpowder over my shoulder again and began the grueling march back to the shed. We replaced my Granddad's property and I dusted off my hands. What an exciting day it had been! This trip just couldn't get any better.

When the long weekend came to an end, we had to pack up and make ready for the five-hour car ride back home. It was important to shut up the Ranch house properly. As I waited on the front porch for Dad to finish, I could hear the familiar cooing of the mourning doves. I noticed they always appeared in pairs. Peace filled my heart as I stood still and listened. *Why do doves sing?* I thought.

We closed up the Ranch, and in several hours I was back in my home town, stumbling sleepily into our house with the bags and books I had taken along. It suddenly hit me how very dreadful it was to be back home. I had slipped off my shoes as usual and put on the special tennis shoes that I was always required to wear inside the house. I let out a deep, silent sigh like the soft, slow cooing of the mourning doves I had heard at the Ranch. The memory of the low, peaceful sound of their singing and cooing to

each other echoed comfortingly in my ears, drowning out
Mom and Dad as they bickered in the kitchen. I started
thinking of the song "Precious Lord"; I had all the words
memorized, as I did to all my favorite hymns.

> Through the storm, through the night,
> lead me on to the light.
> Precious Lord, take my hand,
> lead me home.

I slipped quietly back into my bedroom and lay
down on my yellow comforter. Then I sat up with a jerk,
remembering: *I'm not allowed to actually sit on my
comforter, ever!* I slid off the bed onto the carpet below and
leaned my head back against my bed frame. After a few
minutes I crawled over into my closet and hid underneath
my hanging clothes. I looked through the vent into the
hallway and began reading my book, keeping one eye open
for whatever might happen. I was very sad to be home and
back into the routine of fear, but at least I had church to
look forward to—and Ann. I would get to see Ann again
very soon. I had missed her over the holidays and during
our trip to the Ranch. Everything in life seemed so bittersweet sometimes!

I was sad that Dad had to listen to all that yelling. I knew
he was humiliated like me, but he didn't know that I was
also humiliated in the same way. I had little hope of ever
having a real conversation with my dad; Mom would see
to that! Dad would soon be off to the office, and everyone
would go back to their normal routines. The prospect of
making the daily mini-blind adjustments loomed in the
back of my mind, and I blinked, as if I could shut out the
world of our confined space with a blink of my eyes.

I wondered how Mom got by without us to do everything for her. Then I willed my thoughts back to my book and was soon lost in my own world. I would have all day tomorrow to think about chores.

Estella at age 7.

2ⁿᵈ Grade Easter Egg Hunt, with Gabriel (5) and best friend Lauren.

On the Easter Egg Hunt.

The Easter Egg Hunt with Lauren.

Lauren and Estella, age 7.

Above and right: Scenes from Lauren's birthday party.

Estella at 8 with best friends Lindsey, Lauren, and Madison.

Estella at age 8 with parents.

A family: Estella's parents, brother Gabriel (11), and herself (13).

Above: Estella at 15, with her brother (13). Right: Estella at 15.

Gabriel (13) and Estella (15).

Thanksgiving dinner: Cousin Michelle with Estella at 17.

16

Journalist and Handmaid

It had been several days since our return from the Ranch. I sat down to play "catch up" with my journal.

January 14

My dad took Gabriel and me to Granddad's Ranch in Leakey. It was different this time. I had a blast, but I missed Vulture Valley. Gabriel and I found this old, old, old bike of Mom's and rode it down a hill close to the Ranch house. Gabriel and I also found a hunter's tree fort. We put in new wood and I built a swing and put it up in the tree. We played mostly in the Canyon this time instead of the Dam. We left Sunday. From Junction to San Angelo we rode on solid ice behind a truck at 35 miles an hour. We got home at 11 p.m. Our Ranch is pretty.

I found out that for our ballet recital we are doing "Wind Beneath My Wings." It is one of my favorite songs. Today I have piano, and yesterday I had bell choir. We are moving right along with that.

Mom is worried about Gabriel and his school. He just can't seem to learn English. She is stressed out right now. Other than that, I seem to be doing okay. Sometimes my wrist scares me. It doesn't hurt as much, but when it does hurt, it hurts bad. I haven't seen my friend Rebekah or Kay and Elizabeth for a while, but Madison and I have been seeing a lot of each other. My school is doing fine… or great. Dad's going to Midland today. He's been sick and really weak lately.

Love, Estella

It was cold this time of year, and I stood shivering in my bedroom. Mom kept the heat turned way down in the winter, always claiming to be hot. The thermostat was still set at the usual fifty degrees; I stared at it, wishing I could change it, but I didn't dare. Mom would skin me alive for sure if I dared to move the little red needle past the point. Every day Dad would come home for lunch, walk to the coat closet, take out a jacket or sweater, hat, and gloves, and put them all on so he could be comfortable indoors. I was amazed. *It's colder inside this house than it is outside,* I thought.

Other thoughts raced through my mind, like how Mom always walked around in one of Dad's torn-up old white T-shirts because she was hot, while the rest of us wore mittens to keep our fingers from freezing. Mom was very conscious of the heating bill: the goal was to keep all costs down. Lights and heat were to be used at a bare minimum, always! Meanwhile Mom and Dad kept hundred-dollar bills in the deadbolted closet. *I guess this is how they manage to save so much,* I mused.

January 20

Last Friday we all went to Lubbock for a homeschool legal defense meeting. Children weren't allowed for the first three hours, so Gabriel and I got to stay at the Science Spectrum from 2:15-5:15. Kelly, a Texas Tech camp counselor, came and saw me at the Science Spectrum. That was really neat!

Kris told me to stop babysitting for now until she gets her schedule straightened out. I also found out that Tim Thornton and his family will be moving in two weeks. I am very sad that Tim will not be my bell choir teacher anymore. I jammed a finger on my right hand, so my handwriting is a little messy. But everything seems to be okay. I'm glad I have such a good spiritual couple as my Sunday School teacher at First Baptist Church. I have good youth group directors too.

February 2

We rang bells last Sunday. We rang three songs. Tim Thornton went all out on our songs since it was the last time we would ring bells with him. Mom and Dad both came and saw me ring bells.

I talked to Kris, and she said the reason why I can't babysit for now is because she needs someone from 3-7 Mon., Tues., and Wed. and she knew that my Mom wouldn't let me babysit that long because I'm so busy.

I have really been working hard on our finale for ballet and "Wind Beneath My Wings." We don't have a tap dance to do right now. Piano is coming along very well and I am memorizing lots of songs (10, actually) for the Guild Auditions this year.

Dad and Gabriel and a couple of friends are all going fishing on the Pecos River at the end of the month.

February 22

On February 9, Everett Bender drove me up to Amarillo where I spent Tuesday, Wednesday, and Thursday with Great-Grammie and Reuben. I had a great time! We went to an old folks' Valentine Party. We also saw "The Muppet Christmas Carol." Then Friday at 11:30, Great-Grammie drove Reuben and me down to Lubbock where we stayed at a relative's house named O'Neill. They have a grandson named Clifton, who spent the night with his grandparents just so he could play with me longer. I'm seven months older than he is. We played in his tree fort, saw how far we could hit the croquet balls across the yard, and had lots of fun pushing each other in this thing shaped like a lawnmower. Then Friday night we climbed up on the shed roof and watched the stars. Saturday morning we played even harder. Then we said goodbye, and Great-Grammie, Reuben, Mom, Dad, Gabriel, and I all met at El Chicos for lunch. Finally, Gabriel and I said goodbye to Great-Grammie and Reuben and went skating at Skate Ranch. At 9:00 Mom, Dad, Gabriel, and I all went home.

I had bell choir Wednesday. We had a new teacher and she was really good. The children's choir are doing Kids Praise 9 this year and I might get a lead part with a solo again. We started our tap dance last Monday. I have dance today and I can't wait.

P.S. I don't really write this bad, I'm just in a hurry when I write in my journal.

P.P.S. Dad and Gabriel's fishing trip was postponed until next weekend.

March 1

My finger hasn't healed yet and is still really swollen. I sent Polly a Tech Form so we could be roommates and have Kelly as our counselor. Dad took me to the Symphony at the end of February. I'm glad Dad took me; it was really good. I'm now praying that I get to be Charity in Kids Praise 9 this year. Gabriel and I are going to the Ranch again from March 6th–9th. There is no bell choir this week because of Spring Break.

March 24

About a week ago I ran the dishes through the dishwasher without any soap. Fortunately it was mostly dishes left from making snack mix. I pray to God that the hot water sanitized everything. Mom likes to put the soap in five minutes after the dishwasher has started in order to give the water a chance to get hot.

I had a really nice Spring Break. At the Ranch, Gabriel was swinging on a dead tree limb by rope and it broke off, landing on the both of us and knocking the breath out of me. But it was fun! We had a blast in our new tree fort by the Ranch house. We nailed boards up to provide a place to sit and to give us a new swing. We painted them with Granddad's hunter green paint from the shed.

Dance is coming along great and so is piano. I started tennis at church every Monday night from 7–8 p.m.

March 31

Today is Wednesday, so I have bell choir and dinner at church. Granddad came to Vulture Valley to see Mom and us, and stayed from Saturday to Tuesday. It was lots of fun. He did quite a bit of chemistry with us and taught Gabriel and me about formulas like Cl_2, Mg, etc. He spoke at church Sunday, and at 2 p.m. Mom, Dad, and Gabriel and I all went to Lynda's wedding. She married Jeff and will soon be moving to San Marcos.

My finger has not healed up and I continue to keep a splint on it at all times, even during my bath. It gives me trouble during piano because my finger slips around and makes this tapping sound. It also aches most of the time. I remembered slamming the same finger in our courtyard door leading into the garage a week before I rolled over on it and crushed it under my knee. That was three months ago. It is still swollen. We think it was fractured.

Recently, at Lynda's wedding, I saw my old teachers. They all commented on how much I had grown up. School is fine and dance is moving along wonderfully. Grace's baby is due at the end of May. I will have two little girls and one little boy to babysit then.

Love, Estella

I stopped writing. My hands would get so tired, but I loved writing. It was also the best way for me to learn. If I saw something—anything—on paper, I could remember it easily. I would write out my spelling words countless times every week so that I would never forget what I was learning.

I closed my hands into a tight fist and then released them. *My hands are tired from doing so many dishes,* I thought, *and cleaning; my hands are sore from scrubbing toilets and tubs.* Hearing footsteps coming down the hallway, I grabbed my journal, shoved it quickly into a drawer, and pretended to be busy organizing my desk.

"Estella," Mom snapped, "you are supposed to be picking up the kitchen right now. Go!" I jumped up and dashed lightning-swift into the kitchen, where I began putting empty jars up into the cabinets. Mom always drank out of jars. We had plenty of glasses; I never quite understood why the jars were preferred. She especially liked the ones with handles.

"These are good for me to grasp with my weak, weak hands," she would say. I thought about how frail Mom seemed generally, although she didn't seem at all frail when she was jerking me around the house. I picked up a knife that I had carefully hand-washed, and pointed it down as I walked up to the knife drawer. Mom was standing in the way. I shuddered; I never ever knew what to do at times like this, and felt stupid. If I stopped working, I might be punished, but if I interrupted her thought, she might get angry. I moved a little closer to the knife drawer and waited and watched as she slowly inched over to the right. *Yay! I can open the drawer without having to ask her to move. Yes!* I was so relieved, I whipped open the drawer, flung the knife in, and quickly shut it before Mom could even think to move back to where she had been standing before.

"Your response time is so slow, Estella. Stay next to me at all times. Work right here, because this is where I'm standing right now," barked Mom. I began to wipe off the counter in front of us with my raggedy old sponge, passing over the surface repeatedly to make sure it was perfectly clean.

Mom turned to me then, and coolly and calmly made a statement that surprised me.

"If you ever leave me, if you ever, *ever* leave me, then I will cut you off without a cent and you will come crawling back to me." I looked down at the cabinet, afraid to meet Mom's eyes while she was talking that way to me. I felt confused. *Why would I ever leave? Where would I go if I did leave? I would just be on the street,* I thought to myself. The street was a very dangerous place. I would be alone and in dark places, out in the cold. I would never do that to myself. I would stay with Mom forever even if it meant being her eternal slave.

"Go clean my bathroom, and you'd better check when you're done cleaning the toilet to see that you didn't leave a soapy, filmy residue." Mom didn't like it if stuff was cleaned and then not rinsed off. She would take that tired, weak hand of hers and run it down the side of the toilet, and if she felt so much as the tiniest single particle of anything, she would be furious with me. So I always did my best. I grabbed the cleaning bucket and went to the back of the house to do my chores. After a few minutes, I had to stop cleaning to tilt the mini-blinds according to the seasonal schedule, and then I was back to cleaning the bathroom.

I was in the middle of rinsing out the tub; I hated leaning over the tub all the time to rinse it out by hand. I always had to make sure there was not a single speck of "grunge," as Mom called it, left on the inside of the tub. *This is backbreaking work,* I was thinking, when suddenly I felt a jerk of my arm and the familiar piercing of fingernails into my soft flesh.

"Why isn't the radio on?"

"I forgot, Mom. I forgot to turn it back on. I'm sorry."

"How many times have I told you not to defend yourself? I want you listening to educational programs all the time!" Rush Limbaugh was soon blaring in the bathroom, and it did pass the time to hear him speak. Sometimes he was even funny. *I will get smarter listening to Rush,* I thought, *even if I can't work on school stuff right now.* I returned to cleaning the tub. I didn't have to clean the shower; Mom did that herself, whenever she took a shower, during the week. The air in the bathroom was crisp and moist. There was a frosted window over the tub; you couldn't see anything through it, and I was grateful for this because Gabriel and I sometimes ate outside on the driveway while Mom was busy bathing. However, that was only if she didn't keep me with her during her bath.

Each day seemed like the one before. I'd be awakened by Dad around 6 a.m. for early morning chores, mini-blinds, kitchen, breakfast, making beds, Mom working out in the game room. Mom had to work out every day so she could be okay; if she didn't, she would get very sick. Sometimes she would work out at the YMCA. I always appreciated those days, because she would take Gabriel and me with her, and then we could eat from the vending machines if we had managed to get our hands on enough quarters. It was awfully risky, though; Mom always checked our mouths after she finished lifting weights.

Dance class seemed to break the monotony of cleaning and school. I had made a wonderful friend there named DJ. Her personality was inviting: she was very strong and outspoken, and I had never met anyone quite like her. I enjoyed her company.

<u>March 8</u>

Today I have piano. I'm playing ten songs in the Guild this year. Last year I played six. Yesterday I had bell choir and dinner at church. We have a new player now: his name is Charley. This is good, because we had been trying to find more players. I was supposed to get my finger X-rayed, but that didn't work out.

Tuesday was a big day for all my family. First Mom had Garden Club at 9:30. She was catering half the food this time, so we made tiny blueberry-orange muffins, tiny sweet rolls, and cheese crisps. Then Mom got home at 12:15 and we jumped into the Suburban because we had to pick up my friends Kay and Elizabeth, and Gabriel's friends Tom and Zak. My Dad was giving a tour of the courthouse. Judge Moore talked to us for an hour and ten minutes and made up a mock trial with us. Tom was suing his dad for making him paint a fence, and I was Tom's attorney. It was fun. Then we took everyone home, and Mom, Gabriel, and I all went to the chiropractor because Gabriel's knee was messed up and one leg was longer than the other. John, Ann's husband, is going to X-ray Gabriel's knee and back tomorrow at 1:00. Finally, we dined at Furr's for dinner and went home afterward.

P.S. Sunday, Dad's car wouldn't start at church and Mom had to come pick us up. It is fixed now. Monday I got the first half of dance class to myself because the four other girls in my class were at a band concert, so I finished my ballet dance.

I stopped writing. There was so much on my mind. I thought of how Mom had asked me to call everyone in her

Garden Club for her, even though it was her job to make the phone calls every month to remind the ladies of the meeting. I didn't mind making the phone calls, but I always felt embarrassed. I knew the other ladies always wondered why I was the one making the calls instead of Mom. I couldn't explain; I barely understood myself. I just knew that Mom was getting worse, and worse meant that she could rarely talk to people much anymore. She didn't usually come to church with us anymore, either.

I thought of all the wonderful food I had helped cook, and how I didn't get even a single bite. So many foods had been cut out of our life. No more bread; no more milk from the store. No meat, except chicken occasionally at Furr's, and that was only if I pulled off all the fried breading. No more snacks to speak of. No more Cheerios, only cereal that Mom approved. No more pasta, ever! No ice! I hated drinking plain water. Ice helped to mask the taste, but long ago I had been forbidden to open the fridge and freezer, and now Mom had really cracked down. Opening the freezer for ice retrieval would possibly break the seal and was absolutely forbidden.

It was wonderful to get out of the house, though, to be with my friends, even if it was under the pretense of school activities. But the chiropractor's office was my absolute favorite place to go. While Mom and Gabriel were receiving their treatment, I would get to sit with Ann in her office, and she would always hug me and call me "Suggums"; that was her special name for me. I still survived long nights by imagining that Ann was hugging me and telling me she loved me, just like she did whenever I saw her.

I turned out my light and snuggled down into my bed. I loved this time of day because it felt like the only time I had to myself. I was able to rest, and I wanted so badly to be

away; alone in bed, it almost felt like I *was* away. I wanted...
I wanted... well, I wasn't sure what it was, exactly, that I
longed for, but I knew it was far from this place and my
mother.

This was the only time I could steal away from the evil
that seemed to lurk in every corner of my home. I closed
my eyes and imagined spending time with Ann. I tried
to keep my mind on the hug Ann had just given me. The
memory of it would last me the whole week, until I saw her
again at church. I was afraid of the memory ever fading,
but I knew a new memory would soon be there to take its
place.

I thought about the devotional I had read earlier in the
day. I devoured daily devotionals, whatever I could lay my
hands on to nourish and encourage me throughout the day;
I knew that I needed God's word pouring into my heart
every second in order to survive. All day long I read countless Scripture passages and commentaries, even at the risk
of punishment, often hiding my devotional book beneath
my history book or speller so that Mom wouldn't know
what I was really reading. Most of the day, sometimes all
day, I was tied up following Mom around the house with
the cleaning bucket, so time spent alone in my bedroom at
my own desk was priceless. But since I was never allowed
to shut my bedroom door, not even for privacy, I had to
be keenly aware of the barely perceptible sound of Mom's
footsteps down the hall, or the slight clang of door handles
that meant she was on the move.

As I lay in bed with these thoughts drifting through my
mind, I closed my eyes to remember my verse for the day,
Psalm 118:6: "The Lord is at my right hand. I will not fear
what man can do to me." Other translations said, "The Lord
is on my side; I will not fear. What can man do to me?"

I awoke to the sound of Dad's voice summoning me for my morning chores. I slid out of bed and stumbled into my clothes. My clothing situation was nearing desperation; I could hardly believe how far I had fallen in this department. Mom had pulled out old clothes from her own high school days for me to wear. I used to wear beautiful nightgowns given to me by my grandmothers, but now I wore my mom's old goldenrod-colored shirt-and-short set from twenty years ago. Mom never took me shopping. I was allowed to wear clothes given to me by other people, but never while I was cleaning—and I was always cleaning.

I brushed my teeth and flew into the kitchen to put a pot of water on to boil. We had hot cereal seven days a week, year after year. I began cleaning up the kitchen and then marched on into the game room to prepare the area for Mom's daily workout. She had begun to include me in the workout, so now I was lifting weights and exercising on the carpet with her in the mornings if she didn't assign me a job or homework. Next I cranked the mini-blinds to their specified angles. Utterly perishing with boredom, I sang to pass the time away. Hymns were the most helpful in sustaining me, because they had so many different verses and beautiful poetry, and usually spoke of God's deliverance.

"Estella, shut up and quit dancing through the house," Mom yelled from the other room. I kept quiet as Mom clicked on the radio. Paul Harvey was soon blaring; I always liked his "Rest of the Story." Once breakfast and our morning routine was finished, I found myself sitting in the middle of a pile of dirty clothes, sorting them before they were washed. Opening the doors of the laundry room, Gabriel said something and then cussed.

"Gabriel, how dare you say that word! Don't say that awful word."

"Why not? Mom says it all the time!"

I sat in stunned silence. I had never noticed that before, but I knew in my heart that Gabriel was telling the truth. How could I keep him from saying anything bad or wrong when Mom said that stuff all the time?

I returned to sorting clothes, a process whose precise execution was very important to Mom. I had to be very careful never to mix the colors; with all the little piles of separate colors, our laundry room soon looked like the color wheel my mom had in her bedroom. We had a lot of dirty clothes, because Mom had started to dabble in garage sale shopping and would buy random stuff, which I would then have to wash. I stared at my piles: pink, purple, red, black, white, and navy blue. Afterward, I would have to iron all of Dad's dress shirts, the ones he wore to work each day, and during TV shows I would finish darning the socks; heaven forbid I just sit and actually watch anything.

After laundry time, I raced off to do school in my own room until Mom would call me for her bath time. I still read to Mom during her baths, although I was off the hook if she took a shower. But today was bath day; Mom only took a shower once a week.

"Estella, it's time for my bath. Bring your science book."

"Okay," I said, grabbing my book and making my way to the side of the tub as soon as she was in it. I began reading, and had read a chapter when she stopped me.

"Now lie on the floor, Estella, with the book on your stomach, and practice your breathing techniques." I lay down on the floor, carefully positioning my science book on my diaphragm, and watched it slowly rise fall as I took deep breaths. As I mentioned, Mom's bath was the only time she ever had any real conversations with me, but I never knew if she would be in the mood or not. Today, it seemed she was.

"I think your dad will die very soon. What do you think?"

"I think he probably will. That seems to be the message we are all getting." I winced internally at the thought of the words I had just spoken. I felt a sudden longing: I so desperately wanted our family to be okay, and perhaps if some variable in our family could change, even something as tragic as Dad dying, Mom would be okay. Maybe a death in the family would force us out of our rut. I just felt desperate to get along with Mom this very moment, and these occasional bizarre conversations were the only way we seemed able to connect. I decided to share dreams that I'd had about Dad.

"I did have a dream about Dad the other night. He was walking up a hill, and when he passed through a gate, he looked back at me and the gate shut behind him."

"Ahhh. Yes. That makes sense. I'm sure the time of his death is coming soon. Even your father thinks so." This remark made my thoughts race ahead. *I'm sure he wishes it; I sure wish it for myself... I shouldn't think that, though, I know. She's not hitting me now, at least; this alone is a miracle. She isn't on top of me, either. Look at her soft face: she looks like she may even actually like me right now.*

"You know, your grandmother whom you love so much used to be a very wicked person. She did all sorts of evil things and so did all of your other relatives. That's why I don't allow you to spend much time with them. I don't want them to be a bad influence on you. They used to smoke, and..." I closed my ears to the sound of her voice. I didn't want to hear anything bad about the people I loved so much. Besides, I knew that they loved God now, and it didn't really matter what they had done before. *God makes people new,* I thought again, *and forgives them because of Jesus' death on the cross.*

"...that your Dad and I are having trouble in our relationship. He isn't..." continued Mom, oblivious to the fact that my attention was fading in and out because I didn't really understand. Half the time I didn't have a clue what she was talking about, but I nodded my head up and down and attempted the occasional brief reply. I was glad when it was over. Gabriel was lucky that he was a boy and didn't have to put up with these bathroom sessions like I did every day. *I'm glad I can make her feel better, though. She does always seem to feel better for at least a short time after she talks to me like this.*

I quickly scooted out of the bathroom as Mom finally slipped her clothes on. I was surprised to see her put on actual cotton pants and a real shirt; most of the time she was so hot she wore only the same old, loose, worn white T-shirt. When she was dressed, Mom called me and had me follow her into the kitchen.

"Let's work on the Co-op order now. We need to see what we are out of." Mom liked healthy food, but that meant it had to be ordered from the Co-op that Ann ran. I was sure Mom hated me being around Ann, but she was willing to pay that price if it meant she could get Co-op food and treatments from the chiropractor. In this way God used Mom's obsession with health to bless me! Mom ended up buying a lot of items in bulk, so we always had plenty of food; it was ironic that we lived on such meager rations despite a large, fully-stocked freezer in the laundry room and an equally full fridge-freezer combo in the kitchen. Mom clearly loved buying food, but not feeding us with it. In addition to food, the Co-op also carried toothpaste, vitamins, and other miscellaneous items, all of which were on our checklist. After I ran around helping Mom figure out what she was out of, I skipped off to dust the living room.

"Make sure you get into the cracks," Mom reminded me. I ran my hand across the top of the table I had just dusted; I knew I needed to feel absolute smoothness. After dusting, I would vacuum. This sequence was important: Mom had always taught me to dust first, because if I dusted after vacuuming, all the dirt I dusted off would just fall on the floor and stay there. I dusted with a vengeance, then backed up and paused to inspect my own work. I must be merciless to myself, for Mom would come down awfully hard on me if my work was not excellent. I polished the top of the table again, trying to make absolutely sure there were no leftover streaks.

"After you're done with that, come back into the kitchen," Mom ordered. I shuddered. I hated working in the kitchen most of all, because in that room Mom always made me stay right by her side, and that meant I was within arm's reach.

"What would you like for me to do now, Mom?" I asked.

"I want you to get down on your hands and knees and scrub the baseboards in here with the toothbrush. After you've finished the baseboards—oh, I forgot: start at the top of the door frames, because the dirt will run down from there onto the baseboards along the bottom. After that, I want you to clean all the walls in the kitchen with 409 cleaner, and then I would like you to clean the light switch covers. When you've finished all of that, then you may go outside and ride your bicycle."

Yippee! I thought. *I had better hide my supreme joy or else she'll take it away from me.* I quickly began scrubbing diligently with a toothbrush fetched from the cleaning bucket in the laundry room closet. We always kept a slew of toothbrushes in the bucket to use as little cleaning tools. I scrubbed till my fingers were raw. The skin cracked open as I wet my hands again and again, trying to wash and then rinse off the baseboards that lined every edge in the kitchen and eating area. The muddy water dripped down the walls. I tried using less water and less 409 cleaner, but then they didn't look as clean.

Oh, my gosh, I thought, *the paint is coming off.* I scrubbed with less pressure and moved on to the wall. I knew better than to spray the cleaner directly onto the surface; I sprayed my sponge and wiped it across the wall. Little fuzzy pieces of the sponge came off onto the wall, so I changed to an old white rag, but it left still more fuzzies. I hung my head in frustration. Suddenly Mom was behind me. She slapped me across the face.

"Why aren't you working? What is this on the wall? Get the wall cleaned. Your fingerprints are all over the place," she commented in disgust.

"But Mom, the sponge is shedding; I can't help it." Another slap across my face, then another. Again and again she slapped my face, too many times for me to even count. *I love you, I love you, I love you,* I repeated over and over to myself.

"How many times have I told you not to defend yourself?" she scolded. I started to cry. I might still get to ride my bike, but hopes of seeing anyone or visiting the girls I liked to babysit was now out of the question; my face would show marks.

"How many times does she have to tell me not to defend myself?" I blurted, powerless to stop myself; the words seemed to pop out of my mouth before I could even think. *Oh, I'm even thinking too much. I need to just clean, just clean.* Tears streamed down my cheeks as I tried vainly to get the little fuzzies from the cloth and sponge off the wall. The wall looked worse now than when I had started: it had marks on it from where I had washed the dirt away, marks on it from my rag and the 409 cleaner, and trails of dirty water dribbled incessantly down to the floor. I plunged back into the task, with Mom continuing to slap me at intervals. I wondered when Dad would be home, but I didn't want him to see me like this. I would have to hide out in my bedroom for a while until I looked better.

Dad came home for lunch, but I didn't get to see him. I didn't get to eat either. When lunchtime was over, Mom assigned me a different job.

"Take all the silk plants down in the whole house and carefully, very carefully, clean each leaf and petal with a clean, damp cloth," she commanded. The task seemed overwhelming, but it would be worth it once freedom was in sight. I thought of the carefree feeling I got riding my bicycle in the wind. My face had started to clear up already. If I wasn't too red, I would get to visit someone. Besides, my cheeks would look red anyway after riding my bicycle in the wind.

"Estella, you haven't vacuumed yet. Get on it," Mom barked. I hurried through my chores for the day and finally managed to make it outdoors. I had carried out all of Mom's orders, and since she knew I needed at least a little exercise, I was allowed outside after four in the afternoon.

The fresh air flooded all my senses, driving out the smell of cleansers and musty dirt that still lingered in my nostrils. I luxuriated in the mere act of inhaling. Then, jumping onto my bike, I sped off with all the energy I could muster. I pedaled until I was breathless, and having reached the far end of our road I stopped at my friend's house, put the kickstand down, and rang the doorbell. Grace answered the door.

"Estella, the girls are upstairs. You can go play with them if you like," she said, and I skipped merrily upstairs. The girls loved for me to fix their hair and tell them stories, and I loved playing with them. I stayed as long as I safely could, being careful to keep track of the time on my watch, but all too soon it was time for me to go home. I would get into more trouble if I was late. I gave the girls each a hug and said goodbye.

"I wish I could have stayed longer!" I threw over my shoulder as I pedaled furiously away. But the evening wind seemed to catch my words and take them far away.

June 8

Dear Journal,

Today I finished my second day of Bible School with the two- and three-year-old children. I am having so much fun. I ride with Kris at 8:45 after I help with the boys and get Skyler up from his bed. When his mom leaves to go teach her class, I stay with him for a little bit so he will not cry, but when I leave he cries then too. I have to avoid him during Bible School because I can't stay with him all morning and I hate to leave a crying baby with the teacher's helpers. Today I heard him crying during the middle of Bible School, which is unlike him unless he needs something. I just reached in his diaper bag and pulled out his cracker. The teacher never even thought he might be crying because he was hungry. He was as calm as the quiet streams when I said, "Here, give him this. He's probably hungry." He sat happily eating his snack. Turns out the teachers weren't going to feed him for another hour and a half! I felt really good when I immediately fixed the crying problem.

As for the Hastings, I was at their house four different times the week that the baby was born—a boy named Grant. The first time was when I went to visit and Grace was in the hospital with the baby. The second was to play with the girls again. The other two times were to babysit for Grace while she took the baby to the lab to draw his blood because he had jaundice (not serious). Richie was out of town the last half of the baby's first week, so Grace really needed me those last three times. She thanked me and said Audrey and Katelynn enjoyed me very much. Later Audrey told me that she told her Mom I was the bestest babysitter because I was the only one that played with them. Katelynn cries sometimes when I leave her house, and at Bible School. She clings to me when she thinks I'm going to leave her. She plays with me most of the time and is the class clown.

Madison spent the night at our place Sunday and went to Bible School with me today, and Katelynn told Madison she needed to shave her legs. Then she asked a VBS teacher why she had a gold tooth (it looked gold, but was actually just rotten). She proceeded to ask everyone in the class if they had a gold tooth. Her attention span is short during Bible story time; she talks and asks questions all the way through. Today, though, she did pay attention long enough to memorize the verse "Love one another" and to learn that the boy in the picture was Timothy.

Audrey and Katelynn love their baby brother and aren't jealous at all. I got to hold the baby when it was only one week old. Gabriel is at Tech University, having fun I'm sure. Tammy, Clint's mom, is the coordinator for the baby and toddler department. She loves my ballet, and Clint and I fell in love with each other. Anyway, summer is going wonderfully so far.

Love [scratched out word], *Estella*

17

Our Little Secret

One day Gabriel and I climbed to the top of the Mountain behind our house. It was something we often did; we used to spend all our spare time hiking up "our Mountain," and my favorite thing was to stand at the very top and overlook the whole city. On this day, when Gabriel and I had reached the top, I looked out over the city and saw the shadow of a giant hand over my home and most of my little town. I knew this was God's hand, that He was telling me He was with me all the time, and that no matter where I went I would always be with Him. I lingered, enjoying this comforting thought, and then remembered the time.

"Come on, Gabriel. We better head back home. It's time for me to cook dinner."

"Okay, Estella. Let me go in front, because I'm the one with the BB gun. I don't want you getting bit by a rattler."

Rattlesnakes were everywhere around our home, and so widespread that Vulture Valley had an annual Rattlesnake Roundup. Even my poor kitty got bitten by a rattler every year, right on the eye. Fortunately for her, it was more easily treatable in cats than in humans.

As we neared the house, Gabriel pointed his gun at an angle toward the ground and discharged it. Suddenly we heard the sound of shattering glass. We both looked up in horror. The rear window of Dad's car had just been shot out!

"Oh, my Lord," I gasped, my hand over my mouth. For a moment my brother and I stopped breathing.

"Oh, my gosh! The BB must have ricocheted off the side of the house and hit Dad's rear window!"

"Gabriel, what are we going to do? We are dead! We are both *dead!*" I despaired.

"Don't worry, Estella, I know what to do." Sprinting into the garage, Gabriel swiped a pair of Dad's heavy-duty work gloves and put them on his small hands. Then he carefully selected a rock from the dirt mound right next to the driveway and dropped it in the back of Dad's car. *Wow! Pretty bright for a little kid his age,* I thought to myself.

"Quick, Estella! I don't want you to be incriminated, so do exactly as I say. Go in through the front door and go straight into the game room at the far end of the house and stay there with Mom and Dad. It's time for you to cook dinner anyway, and the kitchen is right there too."

"Gabriel, what are you going to do?" I asked.

"It's better if you have no prior knowledge, Estella. Just do it," he commanded. *Always, in his heart, he wants to protect me from Mom,* I thought lovingly.

We walked through the front door into the house. Gabriel went off to the left into his bedroom and sat down at his desk as I went off to the right to be with Mom and

Dad. Suddenly I heard a scream rip from the other end of the house. Mom and Dad sprang up from their positions and started running towards the other part of the house as Gabriel continued to scream and yell.

"Oh, my gosh!" cried Gabriel. "I just heard a crash and the squeal of tires, and I heard someone speeding down our driveway!" he explained frantically to our parents. I had never seen such a performance from my brother. Mom and Dad bolted outside and returned a minute later.

"Someone threw a rock through your father's car window!" Mom exclaimed. "I'm calling the police." An officer soon arrived, and my brother and I looked on as he carefully took the rock and dropped it into a zip-lock bag. I laughed to myself, thinking, *He'll never find any fingerprints on that rock. My brother was smart enough to wear gloves.*

Next thing we knew, Dad was installing a gate across the driveway. Mom and Dad were too frugal to get an automatic gate, so every time Dad came home for lunch he had to stop in front of the gate, get out, unlock the gate, open it, get back in the car, drive through, stop again, get out of the car, and lock the gate back up. This process had to be repeated every time my father left the house or returned. For once in my life I secretly snickered and thought, *Mom and Dad deserve to suffer a little.* Gabriel and I remained true to our promise to each other never to reveal The Secret of that fateful day.

18

Jalapeños, Moldy Cake, and Pinto Beans

Mom found new jobs for me to do in the summer while there was no school. Her latest kick was gardening; I had to grow jalapeño peppers in the backyard, and now they were ready to harvest. *It's too bad I can't just eat these for dinner,* I thought, sighing as I stared at the fruit of all my labor. I picked all the ripe peppers that I could find and carried them into the house.

"You need to deseed each pepper, cut them to various lengths, and place them in suitable quantities into these freezer bags," ordered Mom. I stared at the well-worn zip-lock bags I'd already washed by hand millions of times— at least, it seemed like millions.

"Okay. I'll get right on it," I replied, getting out a cutting board; I knew Mom would freak out if I cut anything directly on the counter. As I chopped, I thought, *If she cared half as much about me as she does about the counters or the guinea pig, my life wouldn't be half so bad.* We had a cute little guinea pig named Smitty. Mom would hit me for some imagined offense and then coo over Smitty as she fed him a mountain of carrot peelings and leftover veggie pieces. *The guinea pig eats better than we do,* I complained to myself. I looked up from my cutting board after positioning a jalapeño pepper and carefully splitting it with the chef's knife. The TV was on, and I was listening while I deseeded and chopped. The program featured Joyce Meyer, and it seemed like all she said was variations on the theme, "This too shall pass. This too shall pass."

Someday this part of my life will pass, I half thought and half prayed as I chopped and cut away more seeds. *Someday, someday, someday this* will *pass. I'm not sure how, Lord, but I know, I just know that you are saying to me right now through the TV message, 'This will pass.'"* I felt encouraged by the words I prayed. Once the message was over, since Mom was out of the kitchen, I clicked off the TV and turned on my favorite cassette tape, one that Mom had made for me by Chopin. As I listened to the passionate yet soothing music of Chopin's preludes, I thought about the encouraging words I had just heard. Meanwhile I continued chopping and chopping for hours until every last jalapeño had been stored away.

Finally, I dropped into bed. I had borrowed Mom's extra CD player, with her permission of course, so that I could sleep to the sound of Chopin all night. The soothing sounds of the "Raindrop" prelude lulled me to sleep, and I felt a deep sense of peace despite the constant threat that hung over my life.

I awoke slowly in the morning. Suddenly, the sound of the music was drowned out by an intense burning sensation in both my hands. I pulled them out from under my pillow and thrust them in the air in front of my face.

"Oh, my gosh. Oh, my gosh. They're burning. They're burning!" Leaping out of bed and into my bathroom I quickly shoved both beet red hands under the cold water faucet. *Oh, my gosh. It's worse. That is just making it worse!* I jerked my hands out from under the water and stared at them in bewilderment. I was in agony. I tried lotion next, jerking the bottle up into my hand as I scanned the list of ingredients, then screaming in pain as the trace of alcohol in it stung my hands. I grabbed the soap and stuck my hands under the cold water again, lathering them up and rinsing them. Afterward I gently patted my hands with a terrycloth towel and proceeded to get dressed for that day's work.

I gritted my teeth as I forced myself to carry out the motions of twisting the mini-blinds and pulling the strings with my throbbing hands. Pulling the triple strand in the kitchen was the most painful of all. Halfway through the day I mentioned calmly to Mom that my hands were burning.

"It's from the jalapeños you chopped up yesterday, Estella. You should have worn gloves," she informed me casually, walking away. If she'd cared about me at all, she could have told me that beforehand! But my hands hurt too much for me to notice the anger I felt; all I could think about was how to possibly make the pain go away. I had heard that sour cream was good for a burning tongue, but Mom didn't allow sour cream in the house. Milk would have been good too, but all we had was the non-fat dry powdered kind. Ice was tempting, but cold water only seemed to accentuate the pain. Besides, I wasn't allowed to open the freezer.

I finally scraped a minute amount of yogurt out of the container, saying a quick prayer that Mom wouldn't notice any of it was missing. The yogurt was barely even creamy, since it too was non-fat, but it did offer temporary relief. It was too risky to reapply, though, so I suffered through the rest of that day and the next before the pain began to subside. It was many days before the redness and burning were completely gone. My mind went back to the promise, "This too shall pass," and I managed to wait it out. From now on, I would always wear gloves when handling jalapeños. Better yet, I hoped I'd never have to see another raw jalapeño pepper again!

Summer slid by. I was so thankful for each moment I could spend outside. Inside seemed hot and stifling, but outside was a different world: I enjoyed riding my bicycle all around my neighborhood, and visited my friend Stefanie way down the street. She was different from myself, quiet and reserved, and her room was always a mess; I couldn't believe how her parents let her keep her room, and they let her have her own TV in there that she could watch anytime. She had a Nintendo hooked up to the TV and sometimes we would play, but I didn't like it much; my game character always died. After a short time Stefanie's house would seem as stifling to me as my own, and I would suggest going outside. However, I liked being indoors long enough to secretly survey the food situation: my friend's mom never cooked, but sometimes food was left out on the counter. One time when we passed the kitchen, my eyes lit up at the sight of leftover cake on the counter.

"Oh, you don't want any of that cake," commented my friend. "It's been sitting out like that for two weeks." I looked curiously at the chocolate cake lined with dark blue and white frosting, and noticed that an abundance of soft fuzzy mold had grown all over it. But I was so hungry! My friend continued walking toward her bedroom, probably to use the bathroom, and I lingered in the kitchen, glancing around quickly to see if anyone was watching. No one was near, so I grabbed the closest knife and gently cut myself a generous piece. No one would miss an old piece of moldy cake. I sank my teeth into the first bite, and at first felt the dried-out crispiness of the stale edge, then tasted the musty moldy part, mingled with a sweetness I rarely had the chance to enjoy. I was so hungry that day, I didn't care how bad the cake tasted. It reminded me a little of the smell of the flowerbeds I tended at home, when I dug down into moist earth: the smell of decayed vegetation. I shuddered and hastily gobbled the piece of cake down to the very last bite, thankful to have something in my stomach; at home, I never knew when my next meal would be. I wiped the cake crumbs away from the corners of my mouth and then darted off to the guest bathroom to investigate the state of my tongue; it would probably be stained blue, but I could rectify that problem. A minute later, my friend returned from the back of the house.

"Let's go outside," I said nervously. I was still afraid she might notice the chunk of cake missing. We left the house for the front yard, and I breathed a sigh of relief as we lost ourselves in climbing trees and scaling walls. I loved to practice my balance, and it would be good preparation for ballet class in the fall. After a while, though, I began to feel bored. I preferred dirt bike riding through the undeveloped parts of the neighborhood with my brother; unlike my friends, I wasn't scared to go fast up and down the steep hills.

"I have to go home now," I said, catching sight of my watch. "My hour is up."

"Okay. I'll see you later."

I pedaled my bike till my heart pounded, determined to make it home on time. I always wanted to wait till the last possible second to return home, but I had to be back at exactly the time prescribed by my mother. I rode my bike up the steep driveway, around to the back of the house, and into the garage, where I jumped off while it was still moving. I leaned it up against the wall of the garage and hurried inside before Mom could accuse me of arriving home late.

"It's time for you to start dinner," she said as soon as I walked through the hallway into the bright white kitchen. It practically sparkled with cleanliness.

"Okay," I said. "What would you like for me to cook tonight?"

"I want you to cook the beans you picked through yesterday," she said firmly.

I thought about the pinto beans I had picked through while watching "Little House on the Prairie"; as usual, Mom had made sure my hands were busy with something productive while watching TV. Picking through beans wasn't that hard, but Mom was so picky about extracting every single imperfect bean that it always took forever to complete the task. I didn't have anything against beans for dinner, but they were just so tasteless, and I was only allowed to use a few dry herbs and garlic. At least I could be as liberal as I wanted with the garlic, since Mom loved it; she always said it was good for us.

Mom flicked on the TV. Now *The Waltons* was on. All day there was a barrage of noise: by day it was Dr. James Dobson, various other pastors giving sermons, Paul Harvey during lunch, and Rush Limbaugh for three hours in the afternoon. Usually I spent the afternoons doing school, but Mom always found an excuse to send me to the kitchen were the radio was blaring something "educational." I turned my attention to the pleasant family life the Waltons seemed to enjoy, and became absorbed in the show. After I had repeatedly washed the beans and placed them in the pot to cook, Mom came back into the kitchen.

"Estella, put some of the jalapeño peppers in the beans. They'll add flavor," she said, handing me the key to the large freezer in the other room. I turned the key and was met by an icy blast as I opened the towering upright freezer. I gazed in awe at all the food stored away. "Estella, hurry up. You're letting all the cold air out."

I slammed the freezer door shut after grabbing one zip-lock bag of carefully chopped jalapeño peppers, which I dumped into the cooking beans. Then I placed the lid on the pot to allow the beans to simmer, and left the kitchen to go rummage through my dresser drawer. I had encouraging words to read, and a need to read them.

"Jesus is a gift to us from the Father and is your satisfaction in this life and for all eternity," I read, followed by the corresponding verse, Ecclesiastes 3:13: "That everyone may eat and drink and find satisfaction in all his toil—this is the gift of God." I knew in my heart that even if I worked all day long doing my very best, only God could give true satisfaction. Satisfaction would only be found in Christ, and was a gift. Eating and drinking was meant to be a gift from him, too. *Too bad Mom doesn't know that,* I thought with a sigh. I read my devotional until I heard yelling in the background.

"Estella, you let the beans boil over! Now you'll have to strip the stove." I groaned inwardly as I thought of having to soak all the different parts of the stove; I hated "stripping" the stove, as Mom put it. I transferred the pinto beans to a new burner, and later on that night, after dinner, I began cleaning the stove. I winced in pain as I plunged my hands, still slightly burning from the jalapeños, into the hot, soapy water. It seemed I would be living with the effects of the jalapeño job for quite a long time.

"This too shall pass. This too shall pass," I repeated out loud as if to convince myself. And as sure as God's word to me that day, Mom, chores, fear, and apprehension did indeed pass for a time, as I set foot on college campus soil for another year of camp.

19

Freedom: Summer Again!

<u>July 4</u>

Dear Journal:

Today is the day after leaving SHWYF, Shake Hands with Your Future, at Texas Tech University. SHWYF is my favorite camp. It was a very memorable experience as usual. I had a wonderful counselor named Alisa Moore. I had an okay roommate. She wasn't a Christian, but we got along just fine. All the kids in my group (there were nine others) were really nice. I finally found someone who could talk faster than I could. She was short and so sweet, and her name was Kate. Besides Kate, the following people were in my counselor group. Aubrey, Kate's roommate, was nice and had that leadership attitude—the funny kind of bossy sense. Karisha was a pretty girl, and Cat was her roommate; she did yoga and was obsessed with Batman. She was also a talented dancer. Cynthia and Hannah and I didn't get to know each other that well. Cynthia hung around with a different crowd, and Hannah went home before the first week was out. In the first place, she had eye problems, and in the second, she didn't make any friends, despite all of us trying to be her friend. Cathy was one of my best friends. She was a Christian, very nice and funny, and her roommate, Molly, was nice too.

Now about my roommate, Jenn: I got to meet her parents, who warned me about their daughter. At first I took it lightheartedly, but nothing prepared me for what was going to happen. She announced that her alarm would go off at 3:00 in the morning so that she could get up and take a shower and then go back to sleep. She had been doing this all her life. My mouth dropped. Then, I calmly started my protest.

Her defense was, "I wake up immediately; you'll never hear me."

I shook my head, saying, "No way." Finally I decided to go over to the counselor's department. I walked into Alisa's room and explained the situation and watched her mouth drop too. Alisa and I talked to Jenn and she agreed to set her alarm for 6:00 instead. It was loud and did wake me up, but college life was hard on all of us, so she gradually set it later and later. By the end of the week, it was set to go off at 6:45. Twice we slept through her alarm as it blared for fifteen minutes. One morning it woke up Cat, who was two doors down and across the hall, but it didn't wake Jenn or myself up.

We had a beach party one night where we had Slip'n'Slides and roasted hot dogs on a grill. It was great.

I met a boy 12 years old, who is real sensitive, sweet, and kind.

Laurie, Buffe, and Alisa were the best women counselors. Buffe is moving to the Carolinas after she gets married and Alisa is getting married also. My classes were Medicine, Microbiology, and Clinical Lab Science. Laurie, the teacher for Lab and Medicine, is a genius researcher. We toured the entire Texas Tech Health Science Center, and got to walk around with badges and lab coats on, too. It was great!

Estella

P.S. I have reading glasses now. Also, Skyler can now clearly say my name, Estella. It is a big deal considering the only things he can say clearly are "Mommy," "Daddy," "no," and now "Estella."

God was truly my anchor, in stormy seas or on calm waters. I read devotionals every day, and anchored my thoughts in God's word. I was especially encouraged by Philemon 1:4–6. "I always thank my God as I remember you in my prayers, because I hear about your faith in the Lord Jesus and your love for all the saints. I pray that you may be active in sharing your faith, so that you will have a good understanding of every good thing we have in Christ."

Jesus, you are my Good Thing! I did have the faith of Christ, because I knew He was within me. He empowered me through each day, whether wonderful or torturous, to love those He had brought into my life. Love was not just a feeling, it was something God gives as the gift of Himself.

Just as the hard times had passed, the good times too would pass. I didn't want to think about that, though. I wanted to enjoy each day of freedom I would experience this summer. Next stop: Dallas.

August 23

Dear Journal,

Summer is over now. I had a wonderful time in Dallas. Gabriel and I spent exactly two weeks with Granddad and Gran and did lots of things. On our second day we went and saw the movie "Dennis the Menace," which was hilarious. We also went to Toys R Us looking for birthday presents. Gran bought me some wonderful sheet music and a Rubik's cube, which I am having a hard time with, and lots of paints for our swirl art machine. We got the paints from the arts and crafts store, because we ran out of the paint that came with the swirl art. Our paints now are ten times better than the three measly dull paints that they give you to start off with. Gabriel was supposed to have gotten roller blades, but Toys R Us was out of them. Now he's not going to get his skates until they come in at the store, and then Gran has to try and get them to him somehow.

We also went ice skating and I learned some new things. I read Sherlock Holmes out of Granddad's big book containing all of Holmes's stories. I read two full-length novels, "A Study in Scarlet" and "The Sign of the Four." I also read three or four adventures. For two days, Abby, who is now a little jabberbox, stayed with Gabriel and me at Gran's house. She is growing up. She likes for me to read to her and she can now say Estella and Gabriel (pronounced Gaybowl). She wanted me to put her to bed twice. I was surprised and touched, because only her Mommy and Daddy and Gran put her to bed, and now me. She had me sing "Itsy Bitsy Spider" and "Jesus Loves Me" and "The Little Children." Only Mommy (my Aunt Jade) sings "Amazing Grace," though; that's what Abby told me when I started to sing that.

Gabriel and I spent the night with Aunt Jade and Uncle Jay. We all went to Putt-Putt Golf, including Abby (for the first time). Boy! Was that ever fun. Gabriel and I set up our play house at Gran and Granddad's house so that Abby could play in it, and how she loves it! She was so excited. We went to a two-day retreat in Fort Worth with Gran and Granddad. The youth went to Six Flags; that was fun. Gabriel and I had already been to Wet 'N' Wild a week before with Gran. Gabriel, my friend, and I stayed at Six Flags all day long. I also got to play with and keep Victoria at the retreat. It was fun.

Well, I guess that's all for the Dallas trip. School has started and I'm being homeschooled again.

Love, Estella

P.S. Audrey and Katelynn are growing up and loving me more than ever. Their baby brother is growing up too. Dance starts soon (Tuesdays 5:30–6:30) and I can't wait! I am determined to go to an art school in Dallas in later years (when I'm fifteen years old) and live with Gran and Granddad. I love ballet and pointe.

20

Goodbye

That night Dad got sick. It was probably hepatitis. Ever since he had taken ill from food at a salad bar, he had struggled off and on with illness—which was one of Mom's reasons for never letting us eat out at restaurants with other people, or even as a family.

Mom had been waiting for a chance like this. My mind flashed back to the dinner my parents had had some time ago with a gentleman I did not know. I had listened behind the little brown doors for just a moment and heard my father say to the man, "I am going to die, and when I do, the ball will be in your court." I gasped as I suddenly realized that it was happening: Dad was dying. If Dad died, maybe there would be hope for Gabriel and me; maybe the trauma would cause Mom to leave us alone. On the other hand, Dad was the only one who loved me; he was kind to me whenever

Mom wasn't around. Why did he have to be the one to die? I felt desperation grip me. I had to be strong for Mom and hope that somehow, if Dad died, it would lead to a better life for my brother and me. Maybe Mom would get remarried, and then she would be happy and not hit us anymore.

Several days passed as Dad worsened. Occasionally I would peek into my brother's room, now occupied by my sick father while Gabriel slept in my room on the trundle bed, to see how Dad was doing. Sunday arrived, and Mom planned to take us to First Baptist Church, where Gabriel and I still went sometimes for Sunday School. I was surprised Mom was taking us on her own, because Dad was always the one to drop us off at church; Mom rarely got out of the house. First Baptist was my favorite church. All my friends where still there, and I missed seeing them now that we attended less regularly.

"You would think she'd just keep us home today, with Dad being so sick," I whispered to my brother.

Mom called us from the kitchen. "Your Dad wants to see you," she said. Gabriel and I walked slowly into his bedroom. Darkness seemed to cloak my father as he lay motion-less in bed. The mini-blinds had been lowered and turned upward to block the light, and in the dimness a strange fog had settled in the room, smelling of death. The room hadn't been cleaned since Dad had taken ill; it was astonishing to look down and see a film of dirt on the dresser surface. Dad called us to come closer.

"I'm dying," he stated plainly. "I will not see you again. Goodbye."

Then Mom came in to whisk us off to church. I sat in Sunday School class going through the motions of looking up Bible verses. Finally, I answered a few questions, and then at the earliest opportunity I raced off downstairs for the church nursery. Children were my solace. Ann didn't go to First Baptist Church any more, and I missed her so much.

After visiting the kids in the nursery, I said goodbye to them and climbed the two long flights of stairs up to the sanctuary to attend the main service, running my hand up the staircase as I thought of all the times I had slid down the banister for fun. The thought of having fun right now was revolting to me. As I stepped on the last stair, I knew in my heart that my life was about to change drastically. I hated goodbyes. Why did people have to say goodbye? Why did we ever have to be torn away from the people that we loved? I loved this grand old church—such a large, spacious place, filled with so much life, so much of my life. Many of my happiest moments had been in this church: Ann, bell choir, Sunday School class, piano playing, Scripture memory verse competitions, choir, dinner and dessert, Vacation Bible School, nursery work, friends, and youth group. I had a strange sense that I was about to have to say goodbye to this place, too. But in heaven, there would be no goodbyes.

I looked down as my eyes blurred with tears. I passed the little bookstore, run by fellow church members, where I had checked out so many books and movies over the years. I had learned so much growing up in this church since the age of nine. I brushed the tears aside and smiled as I entered the sanctuary. *No one must know that I am sad, or else they may ask me why I'm crying,* I thought. I caught up with my brother, and the two of us sat motionless in the sanctuary, too overwhelmed even to think. I felt loneliness creep over me like the fog I had noticed in Dad's sick room. *Oh, God!* was all I could move my lips to say. God knew all that was in my heart. I could rest in that. Soon the service was over and hundreds of people were exiting the building. Mom pulled up in her car to take us home.

After that day, Dad suddenly seemed to pull out of his illness. I wondered in awe how Mom could allow him to come so close to death without even taking him to the doctor. Then I wondered how Dad could allow himself to just lie there on the point of death. Maybe he wanted to die, like me, just to escape.

But after that weekend, even though he recovered physically, something in my father did die. He was never the same again. As if to spite destiny, Mom rarely let me speak to him. She let me know that I would pay dearly if I dared carry on a conversation with Dad in her presence, and she never let me be alone with him. I had to say goodbye to the kind man I had always known. Something had happened, and I knew in my heart that the man I once knew as my father was now gone forever.

September 11

Dear Journal,

The new school year is rolling in. I'm fourteen now, and for my birthday I spent the night with Madison, one of my best friends. It was great. We went to Baskin Robbins for ice cream, then swimming at her house. After Hannah (Madison's sister), Madison, and I got into fresh clothes, we started dinner ourselves because Madison's parents had to go out for the night. We cooked spaghetti and poured spaghetti sauce over it, and had it with leftover chicken, a salad, and garlic toast. The five of us—Sean and his friend, Hannah, Madison, and I—ate by candlelight, and when the boys left the table, we girls talked about old friends and funny times. Then we did one of those special kinds of things you do with good friends: we lay on the trampoline and looked up at the star-filled sky with clouds and a very bright moon, and made things out of the passing clouds. That was the best! Finally we hit the sack, had church the next morning, and then I went home. I feel like I'm growing closer and closer to Madison and Elizabeth; they've become like the sisters I never had. But Madison is starting to care more about her hair and how she looks.

During all that time, Gabriel and Dad were at the Ranch. So Mom and I were alone over my birthday.

Now about this week: on Monday I went to Elizabeth's house to decorate aprons with the other homeschool girls. We each did one, and entered our aprons in the fair. We won first place as a group! Then Elizabeth and her sister, two other girls and their mothers, and I all went to eat at Golden Corral. That was fun. On Tuesday ballet and tap started, with Laurie as my teacher. It is a good class. I talked to my Mom about living in Dallas and taking ballet there, and she said OK, when I'm sixteen or seventeen. I'm not in bell choir at First Baptist Church, because we are now attending First United Methodist Church. We changed churches because Tom Fuller, the pastor, is Kathy Robertson's brother-in-law. I grew up with Kathy's two girls, Hannah and Jenny. Thursdays are piano. Friday morning I went to the fair with Elizabeth and Kay and their family.

I just finished reading "An Old-Fashioned Girl" by Louisa May Alcott. I've also read "Little Women" and "Little Men." "An Old-Fashioned Girl" was wonderful.

I wish I could go live in Polly's world where people are kind and wonderful. It is so different from today's world. Things are always so delightful in Louisa's books—the people's way of life, their clothes, their activities, and their attitudes. Just think, there really was a world like that! Louisa lived that way. I'm always sad when one of her books comes to an end; I want them to keep going and going. I get so into the characters. I feel their feelings and their love, and reading her books makes me want to be as loving and kind as her characters and Louisa May Alcott herself.

Love, Estella

P.S.: I will meet Louisa May Alcott in heaven, because she has Christian writings; plus she could not have been what she was without God as her Savior.

> In Memory of Louisa May Alcott, a God-given author who supplies every one of her readers with a neat and different kind of love and joy.

P.S.S.: I am not much interested in boys. I would rather stick to dance, piano, God, and the other joys of life instead of boys. I did meet a boy at Tech who was one year younger than myself. He asked me to the dance. It's just a friendly, slight relationship. Nothing serious.

Rebekah Harris and her family moved to Georgia.

I can't wait till December when Aunt Jade will have her baby. As soon as he is born, I get to go down for a week or two so that I can take care of Abby.

21

Autumn

I was so glad that a new school year had started; dance helped break up the monotony of each week, and I had made a new friend there named DJ who was different from all my other friends. She talked about my mom and said strange things to me. She was having a hard time herself because of some struggles her parents were going through. *I can't believe she's telling me this stuff about her own family,* I thought. Not that she had really told me that much, but she had admitted openly that her parents were separating. I knew I could never say anything about my family.

One day she was allowed to come over to my house. Mom would never let me go to DJ's house, because she didn't know the family. DJ and I stood in my yellow bedroom in front of a large mirror that hung over my dresser.

"I'm fat," I said matter-of-factly.

"What?! Are you crazy? Fat? *Fat?!* Are you serious? Just look at you!"

"Yeah. I have a big bottom."

"You have got to be kidding me. Just look at *me*, and now look at you." My friend was emphatic. I gazed at our reflections in the mirror, scrutinizing myself next to my friend; I did look reassuringly small in comparison. I reflected on her words long after we walked away from the mirror. Little did she realize how dear they were to me. They were my only connection to realistic body image at the time, given my mother's skewed judgment in such matters, and provided an affirming contrast to her negative remarks.

October 2

Dear Journal,

This morning, for the second Saturday in a row, I took care of Audrey and Katelynn Hastings and baby Grant, who has just turned four months. I babysit them in the morning while Grace and Richie run or go play tennis. Grant is adorable and very good. He has the cutest smile and only cries when he's hungry, needs a diaper change, or is in an uncomfortable position. I am becoming more and more attached to them, and they are becoming more and more attached to me. I miss them even between one Saturday and the next. Audrey and Katelynn and Grant are just like my own children, I love them so! If Mom says yes, then I will be babysitting them again next Saturday.

I am reading "The Diary of Anne Frank." It is a very touching story. I am so moved by her optimism, strength, faith in God, and courage. She is so like me: she's a "chatterbox" (which her mother complains about), she is optimistic, she has mixed feelings toward her mom, she never tells what is actually inside her—and she loves music like me, too. I haven't finished the book, but I'm sad because I already know that she died in a concentration camp only two months before the Allies won. In fact, I would cry about this if I didn't know that she is now in heaven and that I will see her there. I am so moved by her life, feelings, and personality. I keep wanting to jump in and bring her to my world to enjoy all the pleasures of life that have been invented since her time. I have often wondered why God didn't spare the Frank family. When I read books like "The Little Princess," the novels of Louisa May Alcott, and Anne Frank's diary, I feel as though the stories are beyond real life—that everything and everyone's feelings go deeper than the life I live in. When I read Louisa May Alcott's books, I see the selflessness and the way people strive to be kind and loving toward everyone else. It is hard to believe life really was like that at one time (when Louisa lived). I keep thinking it must all be imaginary, but it was real—life was like that, and Jo March was modeled on Louisa's own mother. She was real, and still is! She is in heaven, and I will be meeting her in heaven, and that gives me joy. But it also makes me sad that people and life are not like that outside of my family and a few friends. How I wish everyone in this world was always like Louisa's characters and my life was like theirs. Lots of times I wonder why God gave me what I call a gift to feel and experience so deeply everything I read. Thank you, God, thank you.

Estella

October 6

Dear Journal,

Dance is going very well. I may get to be in the Nutcracker Suite that is coming from Lubbock Civic Center to Vulture Valley in December. They need extra people to dance and be in the party scenes. But in order for me to do that, I have to be the right size for the costume. They will send the size, length, and weight that they need to Laurie, my dance teacher. I am so excited! I hope I am right for it. For my upcoming piano recital, I am playing "Memory" from the musical "Cats". I think it will be the best song I have ever played, one that is anointed by God.

My friendships with Elizabeth and Madison are becoming stronger. I don't know what's going on; I feel like I have the sisters I always wanted. I have this incredible love for them and want to see them as often as I can. I also want to see Audrey, Katelynn, and Grant, who are so dear to me that I can't express how much I love them. I am saving room in my weekly schedule for babysitting by doing no bells this year, only dance and piano. I have been looking after the Hastings children for so long, and Grace told me today what a wonderful babysitter I was and how much the girls love me.

Mom is thinking October is when Dad will go on to heaven. A few weeks ago Dad temporarily lost his eyesight and said that if it had gotten any worse, he would have passed out. The doctor said it was just an eye migraine.

Love, or yours truly, Estella

I shuddered at the memory of the day Dad had lost his eyesight. I had been with him that afternoon. After coming home for lunch he had suddenly gone blind, and had called out to me as his world went black, saying he was afraid he would pass out. I held his hand, hoping anxiously that he would be all right. Mom had been hysterical and had blamed me, claiming Dad was upset because I was always in trouble. She always gave Dad a hard time about me; it was practically all she talked about with him.

Dad had gradually regained his sight, but we were all scared by the event. Afterward, when he had gone to see a doctor, the doctor couldn't find anything wrong and had attributed it all to stress. It looked to me like maybe Mom had been right; I felt bad for all the trouble I was to Dad, and resolved to try harder to be exactly what Mom wanted so that Dad wouldn't be so stressed out.

<u>October 19</u>

Dear Journal,

A lot has happened since I last wrote to you, but just the keep-me-busy kind of things, nothing major.

Tuesday at 5:10 I went to dance as usual. I also went to the YMCA that morning. I was especially sore Tuesday and for the rest of the week. There has been no news on my participation in the Nutcracker, but maybe today Laurie will have heard about the sizes needed. She is doing a very good job with the class, better than all the other teachers I've had. I have told her how much I want to do ballet and make it my life, so she has been helping me with gracefulness and posture, such as keeping my shoulders down. She says I'm a born ballerina because of my height and skinniness. It was a very nice compliment!

I am staying very humble about any compliments, knowing that all thanks goes to God. He made me what I am today and has the power to take it all away as quickly as he formed my body in the womb.

Wednesday night Gabriel had the flu and a temperature of 102, but he was well Friday and able to tour the science building with the rest of us homeschoolers. It was neat. We saw skulls of humans and animals, preserved animals, bones, and slides, and we dissected a roundworm and a frog. Then on Saturday Gabriel and I went to the arts and crafts fair for 1½ hours. We had arranged to meet Elizabeth and Kay's family about halfway through our time there. I bought myself a very pretty shirt with matching earrings, all for only $15. Sunday Gabriel had a relapse of the flu, but today he is fine again.

We had planned to go to Carlsbad Caverns and then to Chatalupe National Park, but the forecast called for hail, rain, etc., so we're going Thursday afternoon. Last weekend the Hastings went to Dallas, so I didn't babysit. This weekend and next they will be out of town, so unless the weather is still bad, Dad, Gabriel, and I are going to Carlsbad.

Until next time, Estella

P.S. I'll be giving a report on Georgia at Family Night in one week, because Rebekah Harris will be in town. Her family will be there also. They are coming down to visit and to attend to other things.

November 8

Dear Journal,

I can't believe how fast the days have flown by!

At the end of October we took a trip to the Guadalupe Mountains. We hiked 3 miles in below-freezing weather and reached Grotto, where I got sick and couldn't eat lunch. I had to hike the 3 miles back to the Suburban with aching legs and a throw-up feeling in my stomach. Dad thanked me for not making him carry me down the mountain! After we drove to White City, where we stayed at a Best Western, I threw up and wasn't well enough to eat until lunch the following day (Saturday). We hiked 1 mile through Carlsbad Caverns, and after that it was back to the Guadalupe Mountains. Despite the bitter cold, freezing fingers and toes, aching muscles, and low energy to walk and climb, I was still cheerful and enjoyed the beautiful fall colors of the delicate leaves as they glistened with the frost. I loved the way the sunlight came beaming through a cut in the mountains, shining on a straight line of fall-struck trees. On our way to the Grotto we came to Pratt Cabin, made of stone, where a couple used to live. At the Grotto there was beautiful scenery, and some small natural caverns.

Anyway, it was all very enjoyable. We couldn't leave Saturday evening, because Dad and I were in no condition to drive, so we had to get up early on Sunday in order to make it home in time for my recital. We ate breakfast at 6:15 a.m. Mountain Time, relieved to find that the only restaurant in White City was open at that hour.

My recital went well. The next weekend we went to Lubbock for Mom's Restaurant Institutional Hotel Management reunion, and I spent the day with Great-Granny Adelaide and Reuben. We all went Christmas shopping and had a blast.

In dance, Christy and I have been asked to do 32 fouette turns in a row, which will be hard, so we are practicing. It will be a great honor, like a solo. Oh— I got asked to homecoming by Charlie Rudinger, a boy I met at First Baptist a year and a half ago in Sunday School class. He's a nice boy, although not handsome, because he is overweight; but I said yes anyway so as not to hurt his feelings. It was my first real date. He gave me a gorgeous mum. It was below thirty with wind chill and my toes froze, but it was so much fun! I got to see Madison march and play.

Saturday was the Co-Op paint class. So far my canvas painting of a horse is beautiful, and so are everyone else's paintings.

Yesterday (Sunday) at 3:30 I babysat for Grace Hastings so that she could run, just in Highland, because Richie was out of town. That was fun. I told her about Mom's idea of going on a trip sometime with the Hastings family so that Grace and Richie could go out and do stuff while I stayed in the hotel room and took care of the three kids. Grace said that was a good idea, and that I was at the prime age where they could take me with them on some trip—like skiing, or in the summer when they go to the coast. She said she would keep it in mind.

I forgot to tell about the short but good trip Gabriel and I took to Abilene to spend the night with Eric and Cynthia while Dad was in Fort Worth. We went to the zoo and a museum, and had a wonderful time.

Aunt Jade is due to have her baby November 10th, but she wants to have it (by C-section) on the 1st, and probably will. Lisa's wedding has been postponed to January or February, and I've been working on the wedding music I'm going to play for it. My favorite is

"Love Story." It has a gorgeous tune. "Whither Thou Goest" is lovely, too.

That's all,

Estella

P.S. My Georgia presentation went great, and I saw Rebekah.

November 26

Dear Journal,

Tuesday, November 9, we went to the Family Life Center to hear the mayor speak. It was fun to listen to him, and I got to spend time with Elizabeth. Then on Thursday I had piano as usual, and that went well. On the 13th was another Co-Op paint class; I finished the painting of the rocking horse for Abby. Then that evening I went to the symphony with Dad. We sat with Elizabeth's grandmother and my friend Kay, and then in the balcony for the last half so that we could watch Larry Wheat's fingers as he played. It was really good. I saw Mrs. Gladden, Aunt Charlotte, and Ann Michaels' parents there too.

On the 16th I babysat for Grace again at 3:30 and had dance at 5:30. Laurie is really working with me and giving me all the hard dance steps. We are having Jody Nix, a famous fiddler, play for our clogging recital, which I am doing great practicing for and am really looking forward to. On the 18th I babysat for Grace again, after piano.

Yesterday was Thanksgiving and it was great. I saw Michelle and her son Armand (cousins on Dad's side). Gabriel, Dad, and I ate Thanksgiving dinner at Grampy and Granny's and the food was excellent, including the pumpkin pie. We celebrated Thanksgiving at home the day before.

Today I practiced piano, read, did chores, and played with Katelynn and Audrey. Grace has asked me to babysit her kids again on the 4th and 5th of December. She is always very sweet and kind to me. Lately I have really grown to like her more than ever, and I am glad of that.

Sincerely, Estella Stone

It was a couple of weeks after this that I was visiting on the phone one evening with my friend DJ. I was relieved to be alone on this occasion; I was rarely allowed to talk on the phone, and when I did, Mom was usually in the same room so I had to be careful of each and every word I spoke. This time, though, she was in her bedroom.

It was dark in the room where I was, and there was something about being in the dark that always made me feel safe from Mom even when I wasn't. DJ was the friend who always spoke her mind, and we had been chatting for quite some time when she began to talk about my Mom.

"She shouldn't always tell you what to do. You have your own life to live. She is so controlling with you."

"I know," I replied, thinking DJ didn't know the half of it. Suddenly Mom came storming from the back of the house. The little brown doors separating the two halves of our U-shaped home struck the dark wooden walls of the living room with a resounding clang, the stainless steel door handles nearly smashing through the walls. I jumped as Mom jerked the phone out of my hand and out of the wall; broken parts of the telephone fell to the white carpeted floor. My hair and the telephone cords seemed to have gotten tangled up together as Mom dragged me into the hallway that led to all the bedrooms. She was hitting my back, but I was preoccupied with what DJ must have thought when Mom had hung up on her. Then my mind filled with that strange sense of terror that accompanies the certain knowledge that your life is over. Soon I found myself on the floor in my bedroom.

"How dare you! How dare you talk about me like that to your friend!" shouted Mom as she struck me across the face. "How could you, after how much I've cared for you and provided everything for you and put up with you all these years! How could you treat me like this, your own mother? You will never have a life now. You think you have no life now? Well, you really *will* have no life after this!" She continued slapping me across the face like she always did, with a ferocity in her eyes that told me the pleasing conversation I had just had with DJ was not worth it.

"You are grounded through Christmas. You can't open any Christmas presents until far into the next year. And since I can no longer trust you, you will not be allowed to be away from me for one single second unless you are with your father." She turned and left the room, flinging my bedroom door open. I was never allowed to close it unless she was in the room with me. I heard the march of her feet as she hunted down my father to inform him what a truly bad and horrible child I was.

December 20

Dear Journal,

It's hard to believe, but there are only four days until Christmas. It is just starting to seem like Christmas because of the cold weather. We decorated the inside of our house, but did not put up a tree or lights yet because Mom has been too sick all month. She is on high-powered antibiotics until Christmas Day. Gabriel has caught whatever she has, and this is his third day. He still has a temperature, but he and Mom are on the mend. I have been sick twice this month already, but they were mild forms.

On November 3rd I spent the night with Madison and watched her march in the parade the next day. Afterward I had a fun time babysitting Audrey, Katelynn, and Grant while Grace and Richie went to a three-hour Sunday School party. On November 8th Aunt Jade had a bouncing baby boy named Caleb! Gran was sick, so she couldn't see him; I was sick too, and couldn't fly down there. My piano teacher Mrs. Lilly's mother-in-law died, so on the 9th I babysat her three-year-old grandson, whose family was visiting on account of the funeral. I kept him for 3 hours while they went to the funeral.

I have spent a good portion of this month in tears. I got grounded for this month because I am selfish, because I talk and act before I think or ask, which has caused havoc in the family, and Mom is sick and tired of me and my slow response time. I have therefore missed all parties and haven't been allowed to babysit for Grace. Mom let me babysit for Mrs. Lilly, because she lives across the street. But I can't go outside or past the wall very often. I didn't get to go to Dallas, and won't be going there for Christmas because Mom and Gabriel are sick. I am so disappointed!

I did go to the Nutcracker Ballet, though. I wasn't in it after all, because the people came from Lubbock to play the part. Yesterday restored my joy, and got me into the Christmas spirit: I spent from 11:15 to 3:45 with Lauren while Dad took care of business in Midland. Lauren and I ate sandwiches at home for lunch and then I helped her and Shayla pick out wallpaper for their new home. It's just an hour from where we live and is a four-bedroom house, bigger than the one they live in now. After 30 minutes of looking at wallpaper, Lauren and I went to the mall and Lauren got a silver James Avery ring for her mom for $37. But then she took the ring back, deciding her mom would much rather have an angel for the Christmas tree. So we found the perfect one for the same price as the ring. Lauren bought another present for her sister, and I bought a blue tree ornament with silver sparkles to match Mom's set of blue Christmas ornaments, as well as a few other things. I gave Lauren a nail care kit for Christmas. Anyway, we had a blast at the mall. Our family has everyone's present wrapped and bought, and it looks like we will have a good family Christmas at home this year—except me, of course, since I'm grounded from Christmas.

Love, Estella

P.S. Lisa and Craig are getting married January 1st, so I will be ready to play the piano then. What fun!

22

The Gun

Dad and I left the house one day to go to Midland. I was rarely allowed to go with Dad, but this time I was, and we left early in the morning. I didn't know until later the dangerous position my brother got himself into. It always seemed like Mom favored him, but he was mistreated too; she slapped him and dragged him around the house much the same way that she did me, just not quite as often. But the tables were turned the day my Dad and I went to Midland. Gabriel told me about it afterward.

Apparently something ticked Mom off, and she thrust Gabriel into her big walk-in closet. Mom kept all kinds of things locked away in there. It was pretty spacious and a lot of valuable things were stored in it: money, pictures of us when we were little, and Mom's jewelry. Her clothes and shoes lined the walls, along with hundreds of VHS tapes, as

Mom was always recording children's shows—which was odd, since she never let us sit down and watch any of them.

Dad and Mom also kept the gun in that closet. We practiced shooting sometimes at the Ranch, and I was a pretty good shot. Of course, shooting my Mom's gun was a lot different from shooting the BB gun I carried around to ward off rattlesnakes. It took all my effort to balance my weight evenly as I pulled the trigger, but I could still hit the bull's eye with it.

Mom never thought about the fact that the gun was locked up in the same place she liked to lock us in. I was now past the age for being locked up; it would have been too kind. Mom knew that keeping me by her side to be slapped constantly was a better way to punish me. Gabriel, however, was still regularly deadbolted into darkness.

As Dad and I frolicked around Midland for the day, Mom came up with a new means of torture: she took the radio from her bathroom and plugged it into an outlet near her closet. The familiar sound of Christian talk radio blasted as she cranked up the volume to the max. Male voices with avid advice bombarded Gabriel continuously for hours and hours as he sat crouching in the darkness, nearly driven to distraction by the incessant blare. He groped at the built-in cabinets surrounding him, and suddenly his hands passed over the case containing the gun we had shot before at the Ranch. Brazen with the sense of power it offered, Gabriel grasped the gun firmly and sat waiting in the dark for the moment when Mom would finally turn the key in the closet lock.

The day stretched on, until finally a glimmer of light showed around the edge of the closet door as Mom slowly turned the deadbolt. In an instant Gabriel had her on the floor of the closet and was on top of her; after years of no resistance, Mom hardly knew what hit her. Gabriel, her precious son, had jumped her! She looked up as she felt the cool barrel of the gun against her forehead hot with wrath.

"I could shoot you right now, and Dad and Estella would be okay!" Gabriel shouted. "If I shot you right now, no one would blame me. No one would blame me if I killed you, and then Estella would be okay!" He jumped off her as if to restrain himself and bolted out of the closet, slamming the door behind him as he turned the key in the lock. Mom must have been surprised to find herself in the situation she had so often placed us in. She reached up and began to gently turn the closet handle, but Gabriel was watching like a hawk.

"Move away from the door! I could still shoot you through the door, and then Dad and Estella would be okay. I can still shoot you through this door!" he said commandingly. Mom remained crouched in her own darkness for the rest of the day as Gabriel waited calmly outside the closet door. Finally, at the close of day, he let her out.

Shortly afterward Dad and I arrived home and walked into the kitchen, the hub of our family's life. Mom had begun preparing dinner. Gabriel, I guessed, was in his room.

"I want a lock put on the gun today," Mom ordered Dad. He always did whatever she said without question. Why should this occasion be any different? A lock was placed on the gun that night, and it was carefully tucked away in its usual place in the closet. Mom deadbolted the master closet and hid the key away in a place only she knew. After that day we were rarely allowed into her closet.

I had kept a journal for quite some time now, hiding it from Mom amongst all my other papers and school books. And just in case she ever found it, I had been very careful about what I had written. I most especially did not want her to become jealous of my friendship with Ann. I also made sure I remembered to include all the times I messed up, so she could feel gratified about having induced proper humility and remorse in me through her punishments. I continued to write in it as the new year got underway.

I also spent a lot of time reading my Bible. A cloud had hung over my head since Christmas, and I felt a new urge to spend more time saturating my mind and heart with Scripture and spiritual nourishment. I read regularly from as many devotional books as possible, and sometimes read my Bible when I was supposed to be doing schoolwork. Since so much of my supposed school time was consumed instead with cleaning, I worked hard at teaching myself, completing my assignments and committing as much as I could to memory. I was grateful that Mom wasn't teaching me anymore. She had taught me algebra, which had been a nightmare: she had hit me constantly through every lesson. I learned so much better when I was allowed to teach myself.

Reading, dance, and music continued to be sources of happiness, spots of light in an otherwise dark landscape. I also drew comfort and encouragement from every opportunity to visit friends. Looking back, I am struck by what a gift from God these pursuits and people were to me. I knew it then, too.

January 1

Dear Journal,
      Well, today is the beginning of a new year, so I may as well start today's entry with a few goals.

By year's end I hope to have successfully completed my May Ballet/Tap recital (which means I will have done 32 fouettes). I also hope that by that time, life around home would become more pleasant, because I will have fully become all that my mom wants me to be.

For Christmas it was as expected: we had no one over and we went nowhere. So all I had by way of relatives for Christmas was Mom, Dad, and Gabriel. We gave Mom an Oster Four-in-One Appliance Center, and I gave her a few other things.

We went to Lisa and Craig's wedding. I got lots of compliments from everyone for my playing, and I really did a good job. It's amazing how much easier it is to play with a book in front of you after you've played in a recital. It took all I could muster to keep from crying when Lisa was wed. I realized today how much I like her. I am very happy that she married Craig, a very nice 35-year-old young man. She is such a mature 19-year-old and is kind, loving, and understanding.

Now about books. I just finished "Eight Cousins" and its sequel "Rose in Bloom" by Louisa May Alcott, and I am awestruck by the godly loving passion shared between the boys and Rose, and by the selflessness of Rose—how she isn't vain or conceited, and how she puts heart, soul, and mind into being a worthy wife. Oh, that I might be as pure! I wish I lived in her time of poetry, when education was so valued and worked for. Read these books again, Estella, when you have grown old, so that you may fully comprehend the joy, pleasure, and saddest passion and feeling that I have enjoyed at age 13 and 14. It is wonderful that Rose bloomed, but it also brings tears to my eyes, for the story has ended! But all has worked out for the better, and I feel great joy.

When I get ready to marry, I should reread "Rose in Bloom" and pattern my life and character after Rose's.

In some ways I feel as if life is wonderful, yet it is so full of tears.

Forever yours, Estella

February 3

Dear Journal,

It has been a month since I have written, and a lot has happened. I may as well start at the first. All of our presents from relatives arrived, since we won't be able to go to Dallas until early March. I got lots of great presents, and I consider myself lucky to have such wonderful grandparents.

For my ballet recital we are dancing to the "Overture of William Tell," commonly known as "The Lone Ranger." It is the classical version and is very pretty. I am so happy, because I can now do eight perfect fouettes. A special guest artist is playing the fiddle for our tap recital. It is a fast-paced clogging song called "The Orange Blossom Special."

On January 10th I started the Co-Op cake decorating class. I baked and iced a rocking horse mold cake, and I think it turned out very well.

Rebekah's 16th birthday was on the 17th and I mailed her a card and letter I made. On the 29th I had a birthday party to go to. The girl is a good but recent friend who just turned 11 years old. Her mom is the one who taught the Co-Op cake decorating class. That evening Dad, Mary Fuller, and I went to the symphony, where a brilliant piano player performed.

About a week ago I went to the chiropractor because of a horrible back and neck ache. Ann runs a rehab center there and I talked to her while I waited for Mom to pick me up. Ann's husband John is the lead chiropractor. I don't think I've mentioned Ann much, but she has been my very good personal friend for many years and we are very close. She is very sweet, and there's something about her that just makes you want to like her. She is 30 years old, young, pretty, and has no kids, and I think that makes her kind of sad. She and John have been married for 10 years. Lots of people tell us we look alike. Once we showed up at church with our hair done the same way, and another time a girl asked Ann if I was her daughter. Even Mom says we are alike in every way. I look forward to seeing Ann again, but our visits are rare because I don't go to the chiropractor much. She and John have started a new church and have a pastor and a building.

Love, Estella

February 20

Dear Journal,

I slept over at Mary Fuller's one night, and we had a blast. First we ate pizza and salad; then we baked a big cookie on a pizza pan. We also filled water balloons and climbed a tree. Breakfast the next morning was good: blueberry and banana nut muffins. We went to Sunday School and church and then we said goodbye. Mary is a wonderful friend.

The day before, Gabriel, Dad, and I went to the Presidential Museum and then to a creationist seminar in Odessa that was excellent. It didn't end until 9:30 or

10 p.m., so we got back home late. We went to the youth rally on the 19th, and that was really good. They served 500 pizzas! I ate with Lana, a lady who works for the chiropractor and is best friends with Ann.

MaryLou has asked me to teach a 30-minute ballet class for ages preschool through first grade at First Baptist Church during Spring Break, on March 15th and 17th. She also wants me to perform on toe for the students at church. I guess I'll toe-dance solo to William Tell. How wonderful! I truly will be dancing for the Lord now! So at 9:30 a.m. I go to church, it starts, and when I am through teaching I will help with the babies until 12:00, then go home.

Love, Estella

April 21

Dear Journal,

It has been too long since I wrote. I've been extremely busy—if not with ballet, piano, and Bible study, then around the house. I'll start with ballet. I will be in eight dances in this year's recital. A girl in the ballet class just below mine had to have bone surgery, and Laurie asked me to fill in for her; it's a Can-Can and a dance called "Oklahoma" with the cutest costumes. Dance is from 4:30 to 6:30 on Tuesdays now. Also, Laurie said the 2½-year-old students can't dance alone on stage, they need someone to do the dance with them. She therefore asked me to start coming Tuesdays at 10 a.m. to learn their dance and get to know the children. That's three hours dancing every Tuesday! It's part of a dream come true.

Guild is coming to us May 19th and I am playing 10 songs. I made up a song and it's a masterpiece that kids think is amazing. My piano teacher thinks it is great and told me to write it down.

That summer was marked by the mysterious, brutal death of two women. O.J. Simpson stood as the accused and was the topic of most news channels. He also became, in a rather twisted way, the focus of Mom's attention for some time. Even years later, she would accuse me of being like him.

23

Summer in Dallas

<u>**August 16**</u>

Dear Journal,

I know it has been 4 months since I wrote you, so I'm going to start afresh and anew, trusting that my life has too. This past year has been the most painful of my life, and many days have passed where I felt so lonely that it made me utterly depressed. I have felt like I had nothing to look forward to except very rare visits with people. I am thankful for family and for friends like Lauren and Madison who have always been so kind and loving to me when I needed them most.

That is all the bad I want to say on the past except that I have to sit out of dance all year.

Gabriel and I just got back from a three-week stay in Dallas with Gran and Granddad. Five days of that time we stayed with Aunt Jade and family, which was wonderful. A detailed account of our trip follows. These yearly trips to Dallas have always meant so much to me, because I love Gran, Granddad, Aunt Jade, Uncle Jay, Abby, and Caleb so passionately. I can't express how great my love is for them all.

Gabriel and I rode to Dallas with Eric, one of my dad's longtime employees, in July.

I stopped journaling and thought about the ice cream Eric had purchased for my brother and me at Dairy Queen. If Mom found out, she would kill us. I was glad to have that treat, but now I lived in fear that Eric might say something to Dad or Mom. It was the kind of hazardous thing that hung over my head like the sword of Damocles every time I secretly deviated one iota from Mom's agenda for me. I went back to writing.

When we arrived, Gran was tired, so Gabriel and I settled in and then visited with her while Eric talked with Granddad. Usually Gran doesn't like to jump right into activities, but the next morning, Saturday, she had a bunch of things planned for us all: a lunch out, an afternoon at the mall, and then a movie. She took Granddad, Gabriel, and me to a fancy Italian restaurant in Northpark. The pizza was like no other that I have ever tasted. After lunch we walked to the movie theater to buy tickets for "The Lion King" an hour early, since we thought they might sell out, and then went back into the mall and looked around before the show.

It was a miracle that Granddad not only went through the mall with us but also to an animated movie. When Aunt Jade heard about it, she said, "What, my dad?!" I can't say Granddad loved the mall part, but I don't think he disliked it as much as he made out; I think he was just trying to prove he was a man by acting like one. He really did enjoy the time with us wherever we were. And if there ever was an animated movie made for Granddad, it was "The Lion King," since it took place in Africa and had a little Swahili (African language) in it.

Sunday we headed to Maybank to Great-Grand-dad's church. My great-uncle, great-aunt, and family were there too. Afterwards we drove to Golden Corral for lunch, then to Great-Granddad's, where Gabriel and I swam in the lake behind the house as far out as the dock. We also had fun sliding down the slippery moss on the slanted cement slabs. Finally, the long day ended and Gran, Granddad, Gabriel, and I piled in the car and drove an hour back home. (Our stays with Gran and Granddad are so special I call their place home too.) I slept on the way.

Monday afternoon John Paul Holt, my first boyfriend, who I met at Tech and who lives 10 minutes from Granddad's house, came over. We busted 250 water balloons on each other.

Tuesday Gran took Gabriel and me to Wet'n'Wild for four hours. One of Gran's friends brought her two grandchildren who had just moved to America from Ireland. Jessica, a girl of 7, went with me everywhere through the water park, and Gabriel took Christopher around who is 10 or 12 years old. We all had a blast.

Wednesday was a day of rest before Abby (3½) and Caleb (8 mos.) came to Gran and Granddad's for a few days. Aunt Jade and Uncle Jay were going to Colorado for a vacation, and Gabriel and I were to take care of the kids. So Thursday morning Gran and I picked them up, and they stayed until Monday night. I took full responsibility for Caleb, feeding him either formula or baby food every two hours. I also took care of all the motherly stuff with Abby, like dressing her, giving her breakfast and her bath, etc. After Aunt Jade and Uncle Jay got back from Colorado and picked up Abby and Caleb, it seemed very quiet and lonely.

Tuesday we went to the mall again, and Gabriel and I bought a Looney Toon glass at the Warner Brothers Store. Gabriel also got his birthday present from Gran at Dillards: two silk shirts.

Wednesday morning Gabriel and Granddad stayed home while Gran and I went shopping for my birthday present, a new dance leotard. We found the perfect one at a Capezio danceware shop that was close by and very big. It was the most beautiful black leotard I had ever seen and cost $28. Afterward we met Granddad and Gabriel at a wonderful Mexican restaurant. I ate a chalupa, a huge round tortilla chip type thing with chili con queso (melted cheese and picante sauce) and guacamole.

Wednesday night Gabriel and I stayed with Aunt Jade and family, and I gave Abby her bath. Thursday morning Aunt Jade and Uncle Jay had to go to work, Abby to school, and Caleb to daycare. Gabriel and I spent the morning watching Abby's movies, made the beds, and cooked our own lunch, and then Gran picked us up to take us to the hotel in Fort Worth where Bob Terrel's camp is, for a family gathering. We met a boy and his sister there and we all went swimming. It was so much fun.

Thursday evening I kept Abby and Caleb in the hotel room because Aunt Jade didn't really want them in the nursery. All went well until she took them both home at 10:00. On Friday all of us kids—Katie, Josh, Gabriel, and I—had fun eating breakfast, lunch, and dinner out together; one waitress was kinda cold to us at first, but was really nice when she found out how sweet we were. She liked us even more after we gave her a three-dollar tip! The four of us swam and ran around together all day. That special time with them will be an experience I'll treasure forever.

Friday night Josh and Gabriel went with the youth group to the Putt-Putt across the street (which Gabriel and I had done the day before) while Katie and I babysat five children. It was like running a nursery! I had asked Katie to help me because I wanted the company, she liked the children a lot, and she knew how to care for them. All the parents were from Granddad's old church, so they trusted us. Besides Caleb and Abby we had Victoria (4) and Rebekah (7), with Rebekah's 2-year-old sister. We all had a wonderful time together. The three older girls were very calm and quiet for us while I fed Caleb and put him to sleep on his pallet on the floor. We had to heat Caleb's bottle by putting it upside down in the little ice bucket and running hot bathtub water over it for 15 minutes; I'm glad we have microwaves now!

After Caleb went down, Katie and I built a huge fort for Abby, Victoria, and Rebekah out of the blankets and chairs. Rebekah's little sister slept for the first two hours, and then her dad showed up and took her. The highlight of our night was listening to the little ladies talk hilariously in the tunnels we had made for them; Victoria gave orders and Abby and Rebekah obeyed. We let them talk audibly instead of whispering, even though Caleb was asleep, because they were all so good and calm when he was awake.

After three hours of fun, we put them all to bed. There were two beds. When I insisted that Victoria get in bed with Abby, Victoria started listing off the things she couldn't sleep without. By the time she finished, she was almost crying, so I used a little psychology.

I said, "Okay. Victoria, you don't have to go to sleep, but would you please lie down with Abby so she can go to sleep with some company? She'll go to sleep if she knows you're with her in bed." It worked. Victoria lay down beside Abby and was asleep before Abby was! Katie and I were proud of having gotten all in bed and asleep at the same time and so easily. Just about then, Caleb woke up restless and uncomfortable, so I took him in my arms and rocked him back to sleep. He never left my arms after that until 12:30 a.m. when Aunt Jade and the other parents came. You'd be surprised at what all you can do with a baby in your arms! But Katie, bless her heart, ran around doing things I couldn't do, including arranging things so that I could totally relax with Caleb in my arms.

Katie and I talked the rest of the time, about what the girls had said and other comical things. Caleb was so comfortable in my arms, he never even stirred. For the last hour Katie and I kept dozing off, so we took turns. Finally, at 12:30, Aunt Jade and Victoria's mom came. Victoria's mom paid Katie and me $10 each. Aunt Jade loved it because it all went so smoothly. Katie and I said our sad goodbyes, hoping we would see each other next year. Gabriel and I went home with Aunt Jade.

Saturday we all stayed in and did necessary things around the house. Sunday we had to leave for church at 8:15. Aunt Jade's church was very nice, and the service was good, although very long. I went to the youth department with Gabriel for the first 45 minutes and then the service started. For the first half of the service I took care of Caleb at the back of the sanctuary. Someone came up to me and told me where the nursery was, thinking I was new and that Caleb was my baby.

Finally, three hours later, church ended and we picked up Abby from the nursery; the worker said she had been wanting me the entire time. Afterward we all headed to Furr's for a nice lunch before going home. Abby and Caleb were both put down for naps, and Gabriel and I played Uno and Mille Bornes with Aunt Jade and Uncle Jay. There is something about playing Uno and Mille Bornes with Aunt Jade; it's just not as fun with anyone else! Just like Skip-Bo is less fun with anyone other than Granny. At 4:45 Uncle Jay took Abby, Gabriel, and me to see "Little Rascals." It was a great show and perfect for Uncle Jay, who still has lots of little boy in him. Abby enjoyed it too.

On Monday Aunt Jade didn't have to work, so after dropping Caleb off at daycare she took Abby, Gabriel, and me to the Discovery Zone, a large indoor playland with lots of slides and ball pits to play in. It's fun for both young and old, and any age from 3 and up can go in. We met Victoria and her mom there, so Gabriel and I chased Abby and Victoria through the place for hours. We ate lunch there too. We had so much fun! I don't think I'll ever outgrow the ball pits at the indoor playland.

Tuesday Aunt Jade left us with Caleb while she went to work. I had fed and dressed him, and got Abby to wear hair clips to preschool by doing her doll's hair with her in the morning; I did one side and she did the other, using her box of hair clips, and after we finished she asked me to put some in her hair. Uncle Jay claimed they would be pulled out before he even got her to school, but surprise, surprise, when Aunt Jade brought Abby home that afternoon, all three clips were still in her hair. It shocked everyone, because Abby had never before let anyone put anything in her hair. During the day, on our own, Gabriel and I busied ourselves cleaning Aunt Jade's house and watching videos, and cooked our own lunch. We had a good time.

That evening Gabriel and I enjoyed our last night with Abby, Caleb, Aunt Jade, and Uncle Jay. We all had a nice dinner together, and then Mom and Dad came to visit. Uncle Jay tried to convince Abby that I had to leave that night, but Abby shook her head determinedly and said "No, Estella is going to stay here and sleep with me always." She walked up to Mom and said, "Aunt Donna, can Estella stay here with me?" Mom shook her head and smiled, saying that I had to go home with them, that she needed me. Abby burst into tears, throwing herself in my arms, and cried for 15 minutes like that, just wailing. I cried a little also. I was going to miss her and Caleb very much. Finally, I had to put her to bed crying, and Gabriel and I left with Mom and Dad for Gran and Granddad's house in Dallas to spend three more days there. We found out the next day that Abby was fine in the morning.

While Mom visited with Granddad one day, I went with Gran to a grandmothers' club where she and two of her friends were performing. Gran's group is called the Joy Bells and they sing good, wholesome songs like "Zippity Doo Dah!" and "Tie a Yellow Ribbon Round the Old Oak Tree." It was a lot of fun. All the grandmothers ooohed and ahhhed over me being such a mature young lady, and I played the piano for them. A young man working in the cafeteria where the club was being held said he had never heard a piano sound so good.

    This marks the end of a wonderful summer in Dallas!

Estella

I stopped writing in my journal for quite some time after that. If Mom ever caught me, I knew she would inspect it word by word. I wrote about all that brought me happiness—which was a risk, because I knew that Mom regarded any perceived source of joy as interfering with her power over me, and could therefore potentially take it away. But I couldn't entirely hide my joy. I would try sometimes to pretend that I wasn't excited about an opportunity to leave the house, but then I would start to feel so ecstatic about getting away from Mom that my happiness leaked out in spite of me.

The pleasure of the summer made the pain of returning home all the worse. The gut-wrenching prospect of waking up each morning to an endless list of chores and slaps in the face was, after such a wonderful summer, itself a slap in the face. The irony was that it was Mom, after all, who had allowed me to go away; she had always provided something very educational for me to do each summer, and I had always found refuge in looking forward to the next activity.

Now she had taken from me the one thing I loved most besides piano and God: ballet. I had cried so much at this bitter disappointment and loss, but I could never admit to that in my journal, just in case Mom ever read it. Then she would gloat. Who knew her reason for denying me this beloved pursuit? Was it sheer cruelty? Or was she afraid of someone seeing the bruises and other marks of her violence on my body? Perhaps it was just that her obsession with cleaning caused the housework to expand indefinitely, crowding out other claims on my time. She certainly wasn't going to do it herself.

It puzzled me that Mom complained so much about all the work she had to do for Gabriel and me, when in fact I was the one doing it because she couldn't manage it. She always said, "Estella, I need you. I need your help. I need you to sew the socks. I need you to do the ironing. I need you to cook dinner." And it was true, Mom did seem very feeble— except for those moments when she was violent towards me. I never engaged in outward rebellion, and worked hard to meet her demands every day. The way she treated my brother and me was bewildering.

In a rare conversation, Gabriel and I talked about this one day while Mom was in the shower. I had been going on with my cleaning, and eventually made my way into the dining room where Gabriel was doing his typing assignment at a small desk in the corner. I dusted slowly, wanting to spend time with my brother. He paused in his typing, and a minute or two later addressed me in a tense whisper.

"Estella, you'll never guess what I've found."

"What?" I whispered back.

"I found a letter here on the computer that Mom wrote to her old friend."

"And you *read* it?" I asked in disbelief. "Gabriel, that's personal. You shouldn't read Mom's stuff."

"Oh, my gosh, Estella!" he burst out, ignoring my protest. "You won't believe what she's saying about us! She's not saying anything specific, but she is making it sound as if we've done something terrible, something really horribly wrong—like we've done drugs or something like that."

"Well, I'm not going to read it," I said. "I don't want to know what Mom said to her." I resumed dusting nervously while Gabriel continued to read the long letter.

"She complained about how hard it is to raise us, like we're horrible children," he reported, clicking out of the letter and returning to his typing assignment. "If Mom is going to say all this bad stuff about us, we might as well actually *do* something bad." He was fuming.

"Gabriel, don't talk like that. You don't mean that. Mom's illness has just gotten so much worse." I was trying to persuade us both with this feeble apologetic for her behavior. But Gabriel was not convinced.

"There is no explanation for the way she acts. What would we tell people if we ever said anything? That she's an alcoholic? She doesn't drink! That she does drugs? She doesn't do drugs. Her behavior is unfathomable."

"I know, Gabriel. But we're not going to tell people. I always heard abuse is when someone breaks your arm, and Mom has never broken my arm. If we said anything to anyone, and then we were forced to go back home, you know Mom would make my life a living hell as long as she possibly could. She would never forgive me, and I don't think I could endure an increase in the terror I already face every day."

Aware that Mom would soon be out of the shower, we cut our conversation short and went outside to complete additional chores. It always seemed as if Mom was lurking around every corner to hear what we were saying, so most of the time Gabriel and I spoke very little to each other until we were excused to go and complete the daily outdoor chores. Sweeping the garage was our biggest outdoor chore right now; lately, Mom seemed extra paranoid about dirt on the garage floor. It was difficult trying to talk to Gabriel when I had to focus intently on achieving a perfectly clean floor. Also, the driveway going into the garage was right outside Mom's bathroom window, and we could never be sure she wasn't listening to our conversation instead of to her radio. So we swept in silence. We virtually never discussed how Mom treated us, because talking about the situation put it beyond denial and made it too real. We would probably do our best to forget the conversation we had just had.

October 6

Dear Journal,

It's time I told all about this terror of a year. I will not hold back. At the first of this year, things caved in. Mom decided that I had a bad attitude and said I was disobeying her all the time. Half is true. But it's not that I had a bad attitude about life, it's that I hated my mother. It has taken a year of God working within me to erase the hate I had for her. I hated her for making Gabriel and me clean all the time, for always correcting Dad, for controlling our lives, and for exaggerating faults I have no control over.

It was also true that I disobeyed and didn't follow her instructions, and for that I have understanding now, much more than I once did. Mom still does all those things I used to hate her for, and will keep doing them as long as she lives, because that is just her personality. I have faced that. Now I have to try and concentrate on what is good about her, not what is bad. Sometimes dislike still floods me because I feel like an old maid at age 15, always home cleaning and working on projects. I have my own life to live, where I will have to do my own work and cleaning; why so much now? I've had more practice than I could ever need! Anyway, my problem now is how to make Mom see how much I've changed, and that it is not within my power to change any more. Mom sees a change, but doesn't see that I am trying my best and have reached the limit of my ability.

I miss babysitting so much, but Mom says she can't handle the pressure of making babysitting decisions. I can't understand that, as I am the one who gives the answer and does the work. So, all I can do is love Mom forever like I love her now; love, pray, and trust in God to change her heart towards my babysitting, pray that she sees the love I have for those children and understands why I love them so much.

The Lord is helping me. I pray that I do my very best around the house. I admit I have faults. I just wish that while Mom is saying, "I don't understand, God, why they are doing this and that to me," and while she is asking her questions, she would see that I am going through the same thing, asking God why he has allowed Mom and Dad to take my life away from me. Yes, I lied, but I have suffered to my maximum. Twice this year I have wanted to kill myself, because life was more than I could bear. Only by God's grace will I make it to January, for life seems to hold less for me now than ever.

The Hastings are renting a house in a different neighborhood right now, while they are waiting for their new home to be built down the street from ours. I will be so happy when they are back in the neighborhood.

Lord, continue to help me and work in and around me and the people I am with.

Love, Estella

talking back/lying
sassing/telling me
"No"/Making
excuses

I *am* selfish because I talk, act before
I think or ask which has caused
havic in the family + Mom is sick
and tired of me and my slow responce
time. I therefore have missed all
Parties and babysitting for ~~——~~
~~——~~ asked to babysit quite a bit
this month too and I can't go outside
or past the Washes very often. I
also didn't get to go to Dallas
and will not be going to Dallas
for Christmas because Mom + ~~——~~
are sick. I am very disappointed
because we aren't going to Dallas for
Christmas. I would say some things
that have happened (I.E. Being grounded)
have made this a very poor Christmas
month, But I did go to the Nutcracker
Ballet. I wasn't in it because the
people came from Lubbock to play the
part. Yesterday restored my joy though
and got me into the Christmas
spirit. I spent from 11:15 - 3:45 with

*After my mother discovered that I kept a journal, she made
corrections in it, such as the one at top right.*

24

I Am Discovered

I had barely signed my name when a sudden chill swept down my back. Before I could even respond, Mom's arms had swept around my body, and with a flick of her wrist she snatched up my precious journal. I had been so caught up in my sorrow, I hadn't noticed the approach of her noiseless footsteps. At the sight of the words I had just written, she began screaming in my face.

"You arrogant little bitch! After all I've done for you!" Gripping me by the arm, she jerked me out of the yellow chair that I sat in every day to do my schoolwork. "I am trying not to pulverize your body," she said as she dragged me out of my bedroom. I was too stunned to reply. How could I have been so careless? How could I let myself be caught off guard like that? Mom thrust me to the floor in her bedroom and hit me again and again. Her otherwise feeble arms rained blow upon blow with a vehemence out of proportion to her slight body. But terrible as it was, the physical punishment was not as bad as what would probably follow; I had already lost so much, but now I feared the worst.

"You will never babysit again. You will not leave this house," Mom said. She would not soon forget that she could no longer trust me even in my own bedroom under her very nose, and was determined to take away my last shred of freedom.

After Mom had exhausted herself with hitting me, she let me go so she could read all the other entries I had written in my journal over the last several years. She picked up a red pen and began marking it up all over with comments like, "Estella was grounded for lying, sneaking, etc. See Mom's version. Estella is selfish."

I raced to my room and flung myself on my yellow bedspread until I remembered I was never allowed to sit or lie on my bed during the day lest I ruin the bedspread. I slid off and dropped to my knees, tears falling on the bright white carpet as I wailed with loud, racking sobs. Looking up across the room I saw my beloved bay window with the metal bars that crisscrossed inside the two panes of glass, and was crazed by the knowledge that I was now trapped forever behind those bars. The invasion of my journal by Mom paled next to the thought that I would never again see the kids I had cared for over the last five years and had come to love so dearly.

It didn't matter anymore what I did. As Mom approached my room again, and Dad came from the other side of the house to see what all the commotion was about, I ran to the window and gripped the mini-blinds whose hourly adjustment had been such a torment to me all these years. Mom stood in my bedroom doorway watching with horror as I flung both arms downward, irreparably bending and crinkling her precious mini-blinds. I had always used my strong arms for cleaning and piano playing; now, in total anguish, I used them to destroy a whole panel of mini-blinds.

Mom dropped to her knees, shrieking, "Noooo!" She too was now in a state of total hysteria. I slumped down in the bay window, my back still to my parents, staring up at the mangled mini-blinds, not believing what I had just done.

What more can she do to me? I thought. She was pounding my body, but I no longer felt it; the pain was all inside, and hurt so much more than any of her blows. I closed my eyes and prayed as she struck me again. *God, let me pass out so that I don't have to feel this searing pain in my heart.* Mom snatched me off the window ledge and began to drag me back down the hallway to her bedroom, where she thrust me to the floor again, praying aloud that evil would leave me. *The real evil is the way Mom is treating me right now,* I thought; it was my first realization that Mom's behavior toward me was actually evil. But I was too beaten down inside to care what she was saying, and I couldn't pray anymore myself. All I could do was groan, knowing that God understood what I could not say. Waves of grief rolled over me, drowning me in sorrow.

I moaned under the weight of Mom's body as she came down on me again, this time with Dad's belt. After a few more minutes, she finally appeared to be just plain worn out and went back to reading the rest of my journal. I would never journal again under this roof! Now I knew beyond doubt that my own mother did not love me or care about me: I had just written about being so heartsick that I was ready to end my own life, and she had almost killed me for it. As I lay there, totally spent, Mom picked me up and threw me down again next to her desk so that I could be near to watch her comb through my journal. Eventually, the day ended and I was sent to bed.

Just about the time you are convinced that you can no longer go on, something happens. I had cried so hard, I didn't have any trouble sleeping that night, and woke refreshed. God had renewed my strength. I found solace in reading and practicing piano; Mom still allowed me to take piano lessons, since my teacher lived just across the street, and I was allowed to go to church and even to play the offertory. But Mom was like a shadow to me. I felt as if I could not escape her any more than I could escape my own shadow.

But as the days grew worse, love for God grew in my heart. I had indeed thought more than once about ending my own life, but as I stared outside my window through the metal bars, like an imprisoned convict, I knew deep down that taking my own life would pierce God's heart because I belonged to him. I was afraid of taking my own life. I didn't want to displease God; I didn't want to hurt him. I also knew that God was powerful, that he was not overwhelmed by the situation and would sustain me.

Every day I resolved to sing my way through whatever the day might bring. Today I would sing my way through mopping the kitchen floor.

"Estella, you didn't sweep the floor after you mopped it," snapped Mom.

"But, Mom, I did sweep it again after I mopped it," I stammered nervously.

"Well, then, why is there still a dark film near the baseboard?" Edging her way closer to me, she pointed to a thin dark line of lint on the white tile floor.

"I'll get a rag and wipe it all up by hand," I answered, scurrying off to the laundry room. Mom followed me to the cabinet where we kept the cleaning bucket and rags, and stood over me, at my back, like an immovable tower.

"Don't defend yourself!" she shouted. Then, cupping her hand and swinging her uplifted arm out of my view, she flung it down on my shoulder with the full force of her body, causing my face to slam into the tall cabinet door. My orbital bone smashed into the hard wooden frame of the door, and my head rebounded off it like a yo-yo.

Mom gasped as she heard the crack of my head meeting the wood. Instantly, my eye began to swell and I could feel a tightness stretching across my face and eyebrow. Once again, I knew I wouldn't be allowed out of the house if this left a mark. I reached down and grabbed the rag.

"Let me look at it," Mom barked as she yanked my body around to face hers. I knew it must be bad, because she didn't say anything else. She walked away, and I stood there hesitating to go back into the kitchen where Dad was. I hated for him to see me this way. Instead I pretended to be buffing the water faucet to a pretty shine in the laundry room; Mom always loved to see a shine on the stainless steel faucets. Examining my reflection in the faucet, I made out a mark over my right eye. After a few minutes I rinsed out the sink and then knew I had to face the kitchen. I looked down as I passed by Dad and bent to finish my work.

I spent the next six weeks in lockdown. Mom wouldn't let me leave the house with the black eye I had acquired. One night I awoke to hear two voices whispering over me. I pretended to be still asleep.

"I think it's broken," Mom said to Dad.

"Yeah, I think so too. It will heal. It will just take time," said Dad. Finally, Mom had broken one of my bones—maybe.

I would never know for sure, because she would never take me to the doctor for something like this. By the time she would allow me to see another living soul, my eye would be healed.

Food was scarce in those days. Mom had slowly pared our diet down to almost nothing, and hunger had become a daily part of life for my brother and me. We had become champions at sneaking food. Church had previously been an important source of supply for us, but now that we had changed churches, that source was gone and things were even more difficult. Mom was in the habit of purchasing items such as bagels, whole wheat pita bread, and tortillas in bulk, but continually withheld food from us, so in the midst of plenty we were constantly undernourished. We ate mostly beans and rice and a few choice vegetables. Mom often fed us strange items for lunch.

"Estella, come get your flax seed oil," she'd say. And I'd tear off a scrap of whole wheat tortilla purchased at the Co-Op, pour some flax seed oil into the little boat I shaped out of it, and grimace as I shoved the awkward mess into my mouth. I'd finally manage to swallow, and chase it down with water. It was the most disgusting thing that Mom made us eat— far worse than the unadorned tuna, for example. Tuna and beans were our only source of protein; Mom had forbidden dairy (except for low-fat yogurt) and meat. Naturally, no processed foods ever crossed the threshold, either.

"Estella, prepare the tuna, please, for lunch," said Mom one day. "Take the tuna and drain it like you always do, and then flake it with your fork. After that you may add some chopped onion." After I had done what she asked, Mom looked over my shoulder to inspect my work. I was now taller than she was.

"You can add a spoonful of yogurt now," she said, turning away to something she was working on: she was always busying herself with cutting coupons or going through piles of papers. I picked up the yogurt Mom had handed me and looked at my brother in disgust. We both hated tuna with yogurt, but it was better than nothing. When Dad came home for lunch, we all ate, each of us receiving part of a whole wheat pita and a spoonful of tuna: one can of tuna didn't go very far. All our food was still measured out to us like this. Everyone got a quarter cup of this or a half cup of that, although half a cup of anything was a rarity.

I spread my spoonful of tuna, yogurt, and onion onto my piece of pita while Paul Harvey blared in the background. Every day seemed the same, and at least Paul Harvey did help to pass the time. This day, however, proved to be different. As soon as Dad had returned to the office, Mom called him up on the phone.

"You'll have to come get her. I can't stand having her here another minute. She constantly defends herself!" Mom slammed the phone down and turned to me. "Pack up your school things. You're going to the office with your father."

I knew Dad would be upset that he had to come all the way back to the house after having just been here for lunch. Soon the front door opened and I hung my head as I went out to Dad's car and climbed in. At his workplace, I entered his spacious office through the side entrance, hoping none of his employees would see my teary face.

"You can do your schoolwork in this office, across from

mine," said Dad as he swung open the door to an empty office. A desk stood near the back of the room, and there were old files piled against the wall. I felt humiliated, but it was a relief to be away from Mom for even a few hours. I unpacked my schoolwork and studied diligently until it was finally time to close up the office. When Dad was ready to leave, I loaded my school books into my bag and went home with him, glad at least to see my brother again.

On another day, Mom decided to keep Gabriel and me home while she went out to scour the town for garage sales. This new hobby of hers offered Gabriel and me some momentary respite from her presence, but not much freedom: she always left us a list of housecleaning assignments. When Mom was a safe distance away, I ran and grabbed her small portable stereo, plugged it into the wall outlet in the living room, and placed my favorite CD in the player: Chopin's Études. I loved the music of Chopin, and was excited about the chance to listen to it turned up high. I blasted it so loud that I could hear it all over the house as I ran around from room to room dusting and sweeping.

I darted to the back of the house to Mom's bedroom to grab one of the cleaning bottles from her desk. She had left the television on, and I froze on my way back out as I saw what was on the screen: a dark scene was playing out in which a young lady was committing suicide by jumping from the top of a building into an empty swimming pool. In that moment, utter despair enveloped me. I had begun contemplating suicide about a year before, mostly in the kitchen as I repeatedly chopped vegetables. Now the thought of ending my own life seemed as near to my heart as Chopin's Etude did blaring in the background. In stunned silence, I clicked the TV off with the remote and walked out of Mom's room. The song on the CD didn't bring me joy anymore.

I had it on repeat, and once it started over, all I could see in my mind was a young girl killing herself. I felt depressed and hopeless. With no more babysitting, ballet, or choir, and unable to attend the church I loved, I no longer had anything to live for. Listening to the music with my mind full of the suicide scene, I could not bring myself to continue cleaning. I stood on the white carpet of the living room, thinking of how I could end all of this pain... now.

"I will never listen to this song again. I'm tired of it," I said to my brother, jabbing the button on the stereo to kill the power. Gabriel kept on with his own chores. I didn't explain; I didn't want my brother to feel the same way I did. I went back to dusting, and was silent the rest of the day.

25

Risks You Take When You're Hungry

Mom was yelling at Dad again.

"Probably about me," I said regretfully to Gabriel.

"Estella, look what I found," he said, grabbing my hand and pulling me into our common sink area.

"What's that?"

"It's a Godiva Chocolate magazine."

"Wow. Look at all that wonderful food. Woah! We should get some for ourselves."

"But how? Mom watches our money like a hawk."

"We could use one of the loose hundred-dollar bills she keeps in the closet."

"Except it's locked."

"I know where she keeps the key. I saw her put it away once after she locked the closet," I told my brother assuredly.

"Yeah, like she won't notice a whole hundred dollars missing."

"Shh! I hear someone coming," I whispered. Gabriel quickly thrust the magazine underneath his mattress.

That night I lay in bed wide-eyed. The wonderful prospect of wangling a secret stash of chocolate had seized my attention. How could we eat it, though, and escape detection? Never mind that: how could we even order it, *and* keep it safe, without Mom knowing? Questions raced through my mind. I curled up and imagined myself with Ann, whom I hadn't seen in such a long time. I missed her so much! With so few comforts these days, I had to use my imagination to eke out some happiness. Closing my eyes, I tried to see Ann in my mind the way I had seen her at church so many times, and imagined her hugging me. I didn't want to sleep; I wanted to imagine myself in a better place. With my favorite music box underneath my pillow, I finally drifted off to the quiet sound of "A Stranger in Paradise," imagining Jesus taking my hand as I heard in my mind the words to the song: "Take my hand. I'm a stranger in Paradise."

The next day, Mom let me stay at home. It was her shower day again, the only time Gabriel and I could talk. He whipped out the chocolate magazine.

"I know what we will do," I said decisively. "We'll tell my piano teacher it's a Christmas present, and she'll think it's a surprise for someone in our family—and it won't be a lie, because it *will* be a present for someone: us. I'll give her the money, and ask her to use her own credit card."

"Yeah, and we can get a hundred Godiva truffles for only $100, because it says here that if we order fifty, we'll get another fifty for free. That's only a dollar a truffle! What a great special!"

We quickly penciled in the order. The next morning, while Mom was completing her workout regimen at the other end of the house, one of us stood watch while the other quietly and quickly unlocked the closet door, grabbed a hundred-dollar bill, and replaced the key in its rightful spot. That week I triumphantly marched to my piano lesson with the order form and the money secretly tucked away. I felt a pang of guilt, but continued to go through with our plan. And sure enough, my piano teacher agreed to place the order with her credit card.

Finally, the day arrived when all one hundred of the anticipated chocolate truffles arrived and I collected them from my piano teacher at my lesson. I hid the boxes amongst my piano books, and as soon as I came through the door at home, I fled to my bedroom and shoved them inside a couple of board games. That night during bath time we each took two truffles and consumed them over the hot, steamy bath water. I figured I could take whatever punishment Mom might mete out for locking the bathroom door during my bath; my reasoning was that if she demanded to be let in, I could always swallow the chocolate and rinse out my mouth before opening the door.

All through that cold December, we each consumed our share of chocolate: fifty truffles each. The taste of rich, creamy chocolate hit my taste buds like a shock wave every time, sliding across my tongue and down the back of my throat as I slid further down into the hot water of my nightly bath. One night it was followed by the sweet, fruity taste of raspberry filling; the next, by Irish cream. I could hardly believe the chocolate was real.

The next day we got rid of the packaging, and I hid chocolate everywhere: in the toes of my shoes on the shoe rack, in board games, between the mattress and box spring.

Any crack or cranny that I thought would elude Mom's attention now housed a delicious morsel of chocolate. Surprisingly, Gabriel and I were never caught with any of it. My piano teacher almost never saw her students' parents, and she never mentioned that special Christmas again. We stretched out the chocolates over forty-nine days.

Winter approached rapidly with Christmas. Mom became more vehement in her open hatred of me. Once the chocolates were gone, I wondered how my brother and I would survive.

Gabriel and I always tried very hard to do what Mom wanted. She always asked a lot of us, and we gave it. But no matter how hard I tried, Mom was rarely happy. Dad had somehow survived his close brush with death; now that it looked like he would actually live, and the tragedy that might have caused a change of heart in Mom was averted, I saw little prospect of deliverance out of the torment we suffered daily. I opened my Bible one day to Psalm 68:19: "Blessed be the Lord, who daily bears our burdens, the God who is our Salvation." I clung to this verse while I cleaned and did my schoolwork. I also took comfort in reading a new series of books Mom had bought for me, the Elsie Dinsmore Series.

Every day I clung to Scripture, singing verse after verse until the sun finally set and I could go to bed. My favorite time was night, when I could lose myself in pleasant thoughts. I still kept my music box under my pillow, too, and fell asleep every night to "A Stranger in Paradise." It seemed that no comfort was without its bitter side, however, for after falling into bed exhausted and staying up half the night savoring the freedom to think, I would be awakened early the next morning for another day of chores and forced labor.

One night I lay sleeping in bed when suddenly I felt a jolt. My eyes fluttered open to see Mom thrashing her arms about wildly. She pulled me out of bed, slapping my face and hitting my upper body as was her custom. Since I wasn't yet fully awake, I collapsed on the floor under the onslaught. Mom jerked me to my feet.

"Get in here," she said.

I didn't dare cry out, lest I wake up Gabriel or Dad—a frightening thought, as Mom would be all the angrier if I caused more trouble for her by doing so.

"You missed several spots again in the kitchen," she said, digging her fingernails into my arm as usual. "You left out that jar. How many times have I told you not to leave things out on the counter?" I moved to put away the jar, but before I could grasp it she jerked me to another part of the kitchen.

"And look at that. Just look at that! You left the dish brush in the wrong position. You have to point it *down* so that the bristles will dry and drain into the sink." I reached out to turn the brush around when I felt another jerk of my arm as she pulled me over to the microwave to point out a streak on its door. This tour of my failures continued for some time until she finally allowed me to stagger back to bed.

I fell into bed and turned on my music box, moving my lips to the soft melody without uttering a word. I missed my Great-Grammie, who had given me the music box; Mom wouldn't let us visit her anymore. *If Great-Grammie knew how much comfort this one little music box brought me, she'd be very surprised,* I thought. She would never dream how much her simple gift meant to me.

Early the next morning, I rose to the sound of Mom storming on and on about her problems with me. Once again I was told to pack my schoolbag and do my work at Dad's office, and I followed him wearily out to the car. At Dad's workplace I took advantage of a few minutes when he was on the phone to sneak off to the break room and see if any food had been stored in the kitchen by the employees. I came up empty, however: Mom was very strict on office policies, and I recalled her telling the employees that they couldn't leave any food lying around.

At lunchtime Dad and I went home, and I had to stay with Mom for the afternoon because Dad was leaving town on business. He'd be gone for a few days, and so would the modicum of protection I always felt in his presence; there would be no motivation for Mom to restrain herself. I shuddered to think of us cooped up alone with Mom, and my brother's face clouded with worry. Everything seemed fine, though—until the next morning, when he and I awoke to a harsh news bulletin from Mom.

"You guys disobeyed me again. You are such horrible children," she declared, utterly without grounds: the day before, we had worked our tails off for her as usual, scrupulously attentive to every detail. "You will not be allowed to eat anything at all today. Both of you go to your rooms and stay there for the entire day. Don't come out." Gabriel went to his room and I went to mine. Again, it was a trade-off, comfort with a price: being confined to my room all day was a relief, because it meant I didn't have to clean under Mom's shadow, but I was lonely as well as hungry, and missed my brother. Who knew how long we would be banned from eating and seeing each other? My heart sank.

That evening Gabriel and I heard loud tones coming from the kitchen. We crept up to the little brown doors and opened them just a crack. We could hear Mom complaining bitterly to Dad on the phone, charging us with something we hadn't even done. I was shocked: Mom was actually making stuff up! After cleaning obediently the previous day, Gabriel and I had spent all of this day hungry in our own rooms, both of us diligently doing our schoolwork. Mom had lied outright.

"They have been so disobedient. I need you at home. You need to come home now to deal with them." I jerked back. Dad was supposed to be gone for days. He had work to do, and now Mom was making him drive back home tonight because of totally fictitious misdeeds on our part? He would be angry.

So were we. Gabriel turned to me in reckless desperation.

"Let's go to Walmart tonight."

"You mean sneak out?"

"I'm starving."

"Me too. All right. Tonight."

"We'll use money from the closet."

Dad came home, but I didn't hear one word of what he said to me. My mind was fixed on the crazy plan my brother and I had concocted. *We have truly lost our minds,* I thought.

"If Mom decides to drag me out of bed to clean the kitchen and finds me gone, we are dead," I said to my brother when we were finally alone.

"Shh," he replied, undeterred.

Instead of getting dressed for bed, I put on as many layers as I could fit on my body. It was a long way to Walmart and it was about 20 degrees outside; on our bicycles it would feel particularly cold. We each lay awake in bed, staring up at the ceiling, waiting until we were sure Mom and Dad were both asleep. After what seemed like hours of sweltering under the covers, at about 2 a.m., Gabriel came into my room. Mom kept the front door deadbolted, and Gabriel's bedroom window had big bars that were screwed into the brick wall and blocked the opening. My room was the only way out, since the bars were attached to the glass and would be lifted out of the way if we could get it open. There were two sets of locks to undo first. I silently unscrewed the ones Mom had installed on the bottom of the window to keep it shut, and then the window's own locks. We slid the glass up, popped out the screen, and stepped through into the flowerbed one after the other, Gabriel leaning the screen up against the wall of the house while I slid the window closed behind us. By the light of the moon I could just make out my bed through the window. I had shoved my three- or four-foot Raggedy Ann doll under the covers, hoping it would allay suspicion if Mom just peeked in. My brother had done the same with his Raggedy Andy.

We raced around to the east side of the house, where we had taken our bikes out of the garage and leaned them up against the house during our evening chores. We walked them to the street, and when we were a safe distance away, we both jumped on and rode furiously through the night. About a block from home, I finally felt brave enough to say something.

"It's freezing out here."

"I can't believe we are actually doing this."

"I know. I pray Mom doesn't get up tonight."

"I can't wait to eat. I'm so, so hungry."

"Me too, Gabriel. I'm starved. We can fill up our backpacks and hide all the food on the Mountain."

"Yeah, and then we can eat during outdoor chore time every evening."

"We can even bring a little food inside and eat during bath time, too." We pedaled to the end of the long street our house was on, and now had to ride down a very steep hill to get to Walmart. This street was four lanes wide, and we had never been allowed to ride our bikes on it before. As we pedaled carefully down the hill, I wondered which would be easier, going down or going back up; we were both strong riders. We covered the 1.3 miles to Walmart fairly quickly, and surveyed the parking lot on our arrival.

"If the security guard stops us, we might look suspicious with our backpacks," said the ever astute Gabriel. "Then we'll tell him we're with one of these motor homes. He'll think we pulled in late, and our parents are just sending us in for a quick grab of groceries."

What a brilliant plan. We parked our bikes away from the door and walked right past a wordless security guard. Then we roamed the store, scooping our favorites: I chose chips, as we hadn't eaten any in forever. We bought $100 worth of food, including chocolate cake, pop tarts, and anything we wanted that we were never allowed to eat. When we got back to our bikes, we put everything into the backpacks and took off back up the steep hill. It was hard work pedaling, and my fingers were beginning to really feel the cold.

"We have to hurry, Gabriel. Every second we're out here is a second Mom could wake up to pull me out of bed. What will we do with the food tonight? We don't have time to bury it. We can't afford the risk," I said.

"We'll just have to hide it somewhere in your closet. Mom doesn't look in your closet very often, because you always keep it so clean," my brother replied, once again demonstrating his keen powers of perception and his grasp of strategy. We reached home, parked our bikes, and walked around to the front of the house where my bedroom was.

This would be the worst part of the night, as there was no way of knowing when to open the window; we would just have to chance it and hope that Mom would not be wandering the house when we snuck back in.

I gently raised the sash and slid in with Gabriel on my heels. He replaced the screen without a sound, and I closed and locked the window. Gabriel scurried off to his own bed while I threw the backpacks onto a shelf in my closet, underneath my clothes. Then I slipped into bed, where I peeled off the layers of clothing under the covers and shoved them between the wall and my bed. I had no sooner succeeded at this than Mom cracked open my bedroom door. I waited breathlessly with eyes closed, hoping she would believe I was still asleep, and soon I heard her move away, probably to check on my brother. I breathed a sigh of relief as I finally heard the slight clang of the little brown doors that meant she was probably going to the kitchen or the workout room. A short time later I fell into a somewhat fitful sleep, restless with the thought of all that hidden food in my closet. I couldn't wait to get it to the Mountain.

In the morning, Mom sent us outside to do chores. I ran out the garage door with the food as soon as I was sure she was actually in the shower; I was really glad she wasn't taking a bath today, or she'd want me stay and read out loud to her. Gabriel and I ran up the Mountain and dug up the cold, hard winter earth, dropped in the backpacks full of food, and covered them up as well as we could to keep the animals out of it. We'd saved a little food to eat later during our nightly bath time, but we couldn't risk keeping too much food out; we would have to make it last as long as we possibly could.

These were the harebrained ways by which we kept ourselves from starving.

26

Building Endurance

Every day during chore time, in the evenings, Gabriel and I would take turns running a short distance up the Mountain to our secret food stash. One of us would always wait below, halfway between the garage door and the place where we had buried our food. We came up with a signal in case Mom suddenly surprised us by coming outside to check on our work: one of us would yell out, "Coming, Mom!" just like we always did when she called us. We didn't want to raise suspicion by doing or saying anything unusual. This signal would alert whoever was with the food to book it down the Mountain. Fortunately, Mom never came out that first week to check on us. Inevitably, though, our well of Walmart food ran dry after about two weeks, and the hunger pains I was so accustomed to feeling returned.

I arrived in the kitchen one morning at the usual time of 7:30, dressed and ready to work. Mom handed me one half of a whole wheat English muffin, a special kind from the Co-Op. No butter or cream cheese was allowed, of course, so with steely resolve I gagged down my dry, crusty half of English muffin as Mom gave me her instructions.

"Estella, I want you to start working out with me every day now. Come on! Time to do aerobics." I groaned inwardly and shot a woeful backward glance at my brother, who had been spared this unpleasant obligation. Mom's daily workout time had been another moment of freedom we usually had the luxury of sharing. Mom never skipped her workout, although sometimes she would start her regimen at around 5 a.m. *Not anymore,* I thought. *She will probably always wait for me now.*

"Get my workout board and place it there for me, then get out the other step board and put it over there for yourself," Mom commanded. I shuddered as I moved to obey. I didn't like getting too close to Mom. I dropped her step board down first.

"That's the wrong spot," she said, adding a slap for emphasis. "Over there." I moved the step board back and closer to the center of the room, right in front of the television. Next, I scooted my own step board between Mom's and the stationary bicycle. There was also a weight machine in the room, and a lot of loose weights ranging from 5 to 20 pounds. Some of the weights were made with Velcro and Mom called them leg weights.

"Turn the television on and power up the VCR," ordered Mom.

"Yes, Ma'am." I pushed the button on the front of the television.

"Aaaughh!" Mom let out a wail of irritation as she lunged at me and hit me on the back.

"What?" I cried out, terrified.

"You aren't supposed to push the button on the TV! You have to use the remote or you will ruin the TV. The buttons on the actual TV are always the first to go. Don't touch them, any of them, ever!" Mom explained in her typical hysterical tone.

"Okay. Okay," I replied softly, to reassure her that I understood. Already shaken, I began to march up and down on the step board and wave my arms to the aerobic video that was now playing. After thirty minutes of vigorous exercise, Mom motioned to the loose weights.

"Strap these onto your legs, and then lift them like this and follow me," she said.

Next came the arm and back workout. Mom got down on one knee and rested her stomach on the other as she demonstrated.

"We lift the weights like this as we squeeze together our shoulder blades. This works a part of the back that is never used or strengthened in normal life," she declared. I continued to do whatever she did.

Gabriel is so lucky! I sighed inwardly as I thought of the whole hour he was having to himself in the back of the house. Finally, the workout was over. After I had cleaned up the workout equipment and turned off the TV and VCR with the remotes, we walked into the kitchen.

"I want you to cut up and grate all of this today," Mom said, gesturing at a pile of unrecognizable vegetable matter on the counter.

"What is it?" I asked. I had never seen anything like it. It was brownish tan in color with little hairs sticking out, and shaped like the earthworms I used to play with on rainy days.

"It's horseradish root," answered Mom.

"Horseradish?" I furrowed my eyebrows, trying to recall the substance. With Mom, you never asked too many questions.

"Use this cutting board," Mom said as she pulled out the built-in cutting board under the large kitchen counter. That was odd; Mom didn't usually let me use this cutting board. She dumped a mountain of the root on the counter in front of me, turned, and walked out of the room toward the back of the house. Unbelievable! I would get a break from having her stand over me while I worked.

I opened the drawer that housed all the used zip-lock bags. I hated washing them, especially once they got old and thin and cloudy like these; it was hard to rinse the suds out. *If I ever have my own home, I am never washing another zip-lock bag as long as I live,* I vowed to myself. Knowing I'd need a lot of bags to store the grated root in, I picked up a wad of them, some still smelling of jalapeño peppers, and dumped them on the counter; then I carefully lined up a couple of roots side by side and used the chef's knife to make my first cut. I started peeling away the outer brown covering. After I'd made several more cuts, I became aware of a stinging pain in each eye. I quickly wiped them with my sleeve and kept cutting as my nose began to drip. Taking another root, I placed it under the knife and then closed my eyes as I made another cut.

I could plunge this knife into my heart and just end it all now, I thought. My mind went back to the disturbing suicide scene that had so traumatized me. The idea was certainly tempting. I was so tired of seeing this knife. Mom had always forbidden me, on pain of death, ever to lay the knife in the sink; she always said it would scratch the white enamel. I thrust the knife, even though it was dirty, into the plastic dish rack.

My eyes were stinging now with almost unbearable pain. I felt a fire inside my face, and the irritation in my nostrils was like a thousand pinpricks. Shutting my eyes tight, I dropped the horseradish and ran to the sink. I tried washing my hands and eyes with cold water, but the stinging persisted—and besides, this interruption would only prolong the job. After pressing a washcloth to both eyes, I went back to my task, keeping the washcloth close by where I could grab it whenever I was too blinded by tears to keep going.

I cut up horseradish for almost two hours. What could Mom possibly want with so much of this root? Tears streamed down my face as I cut, peeled, grated, and then quickly sealed up each little batch of horseradish root. Finally, the last bag was sealed and I placed all the bags next to the locked freezer; I wasn't allowed to open any refrigerator or freezer in our house unless Mom was present. Then I washed the cutting board and knife and tried frantically to clean my face, crying out with pain as I did so: the burning wouldn't stop. I fled from the kitchen to my bedroom in the back of the house, desperately wishing never to see horseradish again.

Grabbing my Bible I flung it open, a haze of printed words swimming before my stinging eyes. The pages had fallen open to John 10:28: "And I give them eternal life, and they shall never perish; neither shall anyone snatch them out of my hand. My Father, who has given them to me, is greater than all; and no one is able to snatch them out of my Father's hand. I and my Father are one." I looked up from my Bible and stared out the window. My gaze was fuzzy, blurring together the crisscrossed bars on each windowpane so as to form an impenetrable fortress. Fortresses were supposed to protect; this one only wounded and oppressed its inhabitants. I contemplated ending my life again.

I could just end it all now, I thought again. *If I don't, I could be locked away here forever. This way of life may go on for a very long time. And I can't run away, because then I would just be on the street and open to attack from everyone.* I closed my eyes, and my thoughts went back to God. *I don't want to make God sad. If I kill myself, it will make God very sad. He doesn't want me to do it; that much I do know. I'm here for good, I guess, and will simply have to endure with God's help. I'm deciding once and for all never to think of this subject again. I'm not killing myself—period!*

27

Gifts from the God Who Sustains

Mom called Dad almost every day during his work hours, even though he was home for breakfast, lunch, and dinner. She called for only one reason: to complain about me. Finally, Mom demanded that Dad take me with him to work several mornings a week.

I felt so humiliated by this in the eyes of my father, I could scarcely speak when I was with him. Every day I sat quietly in the car as we rode together to his work. He never seemed anxious to talk about what was happening, and I didn't know what to say. He saw what my life was like, and since he chose to let me suffer, I didn't think I could change his mind. Though sitting right next to me in the car, he seemed so far away, unreachable. I looked out the window at the blur of trees racing by, and smiled as I thought that God wasn't like that. Through Jesus, God was always reachable.

I could never call my Dad on the phone, or even speak to him when he was around, but I could talk to the Lord any time I wanted. He was only a breath away. That is what he had always told me.

He had whispered this to me during the dark hours at home. *I'm only a breath away. I'm only a breath away.* I knew what that meant: it meant that Jesus was near me and in me through the Holy Spirit. He was invisible and yet real, like the air I breathed every moment of my life, and he would sustain me. After deciding to keep on living, I had felt a fresh peace settle over my heart: God, I knew, had given me the grace to endure.

We pulled into the office parking lot and entered the building, where I sat in my usual place in the vacant office at the end of the hallway. But while plugging away at my schoolwork, I was suddenly gripped with terrible stomach pains, resurrecting distant memories of the oatmeal Mom used to force upon me. She had stopped that years ago; I still ate oatmeal, but it was a different kind that didn't make my stomach hurt. I hadn't had pains like this in a very long time.

"I think I have the stomach flu," I informed Dad. He let me lie down on his office couch and then walked out.

"I have to go run payroll and do some other errands," he said over his shoulder. "I'll be back in 45 minutes." I curled up in the fetal position, gripping my stomach tightly as the cramps intensified.

"I wish I could just go ahead and throw up," I said out loud to the empty wall. The room was dark; Dad had turned out all the lights for me before leaving. "At least I'm not at home," I said to the air. But I knew God was listening. I closed my eyes and began to pray, "Oh God, please deliver me from this pain. Please make me feel better. I just can't be sick when I go home; Mom will kill me if I'm sick. Please take this pain away, Lord. Please!" My voice faded as I drifted off to sleep with stabs of pain in my abdomen.

All at once I found myself walking on pavement along the edge of a parking lot. It was crowded with bystanders to my left; on my right was a beautiful green meadow that looked like a park. There were big trees, and the air smelled fresh. As I walked, an African-American woman close by in the parking lot began to sing in deep, vibrant tones a song I instantly recognized: "Revive Us Again." It was one I had sung often in my childhood at First Baptist Church. The woman's voice boomed with power and vitality, and the beauty of her singing surrounded and penetrated my being. The subtle accompaniment of a choir overhead (were they angels?) added a gentle harmony and fullness. I heard each word sung:

> We praise thee, O God, for the Son of thy love,
> For Jesus who died and is now gone above.
>> *Hallelujah! Thine the glory. Hallelujah! Amen.*
>> *Hallelujah! Thine the glory. Revive us again.*

> We praise thee, O God, for thy Spirit of light,
> Who hath shown us our Savior, and scattered
>> our night.

> All glory and praise to the Lamb that was slain,
> Who hath borne all our sins, and hath cleansed
>> every stain.

> All glory and praise to the God of all grace,
> Who hast brought us, and sought us, and
>> guided our ways.

Revive us again; fill each heart with thy love.
May each soul be rekindled with fire from above.
Hallelujah! Thine the glory. Hallelujah! Amen.
Hallelujah! Thine the glory. Revive us again.

I opened my eyes and looked over at the clock in Dad's office. I was surprised; only thirty minutes had passed. I noticed immediately that my stomach was completely well, and knew that God had healed me. He had touched me in a way that He knew would bless me, through music and the sound of singing.

"You are so sweet that way," I whispered to Jesus. "You always touch me in a way that is special to me." In the few minutes before Dad returned to take me home (Mom usually sent me to the office for only part of the day), I sat contemplating the incredible thing God had just done for me. When we arrived home, Dad made no mention of my illness to Mom, and I breathed another prayer of thanksgiving to Jesus.

Spring was around the corner, but the days seemed to pass so slowly. Every day I did the same things: Mom had me work out with her in the mornings, or go to the office with Dad to do my schoolwork. I was fifteen, and Mom and I still did not get along. It frustrated me that I could never seem to say the right thing to her and that none of my efforts to please her succeeded. I continued with my piano, pouring all my emotions into music by my favorite composer, Chopin. The conductor of the symphony had asked me to play a piano concerto with the orchestra, and for this reason alone Mom was allowing me out of the house. I worked diligently to improve my musical skills in between chores and schoolwork; I could have played piano all day if Mom had let me. Now the fact that I was playing with the symphony helped to boost the amount of time I was allowed to step away from chores in order to practice. Although she still limited my practice time, Mom seemed to really want me to excel at the piano. For this too I was grateful.

Finally, the day of the performance arrived. I stepped onto the stage, arrayed in a long, crisp white dress with pink rosebuds and green leaves embroidered on the edge; I had starched and ironed it to perfection. Sitting at the piano, I placed my fingers on the brilliant white ivory keys while behind me the orchestra exploded into music, drawing me with it into another world. I played passionately and well, right to the cadenza at the end. This ending was a solo part featuring special techniques on the keyboard, a challenging passage even for a master pianist. After my performance I smiled and bowed, happy with myself and the opportunity God had afforded me. The crowd was so pleased, I had to walk back on stage more than once, each time looking out into the audience for friends and loved ones; my best friend Lauren was out there somewhere. I found her afterwards and had a few minutes to visit with her before she returned to her home in Midland with her mother. I was glad my family had invited them. They all ended up in the balcony, because my mother arrived late.

Once my performance was finished, Mom barely spoke. I knew she must be crazed with jealousy. She hardly acknowledged the presence of Lauren's mother, or even my presence, for that matter. But I was so glad to have a chance to speak with Lauren for a few moments; she had been my best friend since I was six years old. I knew she could read the deep sadness in my eyes, although I didn't dare breathe a word against Mom, or about the horrors I would return to at home now that my fairy-tale performance was over. I took a deep breath and resolved to enjoy these few minutes with my friend. Lauren's mother told me what an incredible performance I had given and how proud she was of me, and I beamed as I thought of the packed hall filled with hundreds of people.

When the time came to say goodbye, I hugged my best friend and steeled myself for the return to reality. It was time to go back to prison. God and God alone knew when or if I would get to leave home again.

28

This Too Shall Pass

Mom's distaste for me was growing. She simply could not stand me, and at the same time she could not stand to have me away from her side and out of her control. She needed me, but didn't want me. She couldn't live with me, and she couldn't live without me. She needed someone to blame for every mishap in her life, and I guess I was that someone. I wondered what she would have done without me as her punching bag. But even after fifteen long years, I had under-estimated Mom's capacity for hurting me.

Mom announced one day, to my surprise, that I was to go out with her. She never took me anywhere anymore, not after what had happened at the grocery store: Mom had taken me to Walmart to help her shop for groceries, and every time she so much as raised her arm to grab a vegetable from the produce stand, I had jumped or flinched violently, so accustomed was I to her incessant hitting and slapping at home. By the time we got back to the car, Mom was wild with anger.

"Why did you keep jumping?" she yelled. "Why did you flinch like that? I can't take you anywhere, *anywhere!*" After that she quit going into the grocery store herself. She would make Dad go, or have Dad take me and send me in to get groceries. I was grateful for this, as it gave me extra moments away from Mom. It was funny how God used the bad to work out for my good just like he said in Romans 8:28: "For we know that all things work together for good to those who love God, to those who are called according to His purpose."

One day Mom seemed particularly upset with me for defending myself, meaning that I had met her unjust accusations with reasons for my actions.

"Grab the cleaning bucket, vacuum, broom, mop, and plenty of rags," she barked, "and come with me." I did as she said and climbed into the car after her, loaded with the cleaning supplies. We drove to another part of town and pulled into the parking lot of an apartment complex, where Mom got out of the car and commanded me to follow suit. She inserted a key into the lock of a ground floor apartment, and we walked into a bare room. I looked around at carpet, walls, and baseboards. There was no furniture.

"Estella, you are to clean this place from top to bottom, ceiling to floor. Scrub every crack with the toothbrushes. You are to have no food. If you go across the street to get food from the gas station, I will kill you. You can drink the water from the sink. I'm locking you in so there is no way for you to get out. Do not leave. If you do, I will know." With that she turned and walked out, locking the door behind her with the only key.

I stood in stunned silence at first, barely able to move. I was already hungry, and Mom probably wouldn't be back until the next day. There was no TV, no radio, no CD player, no way to pass the time, and no phone to call anyone to bring me something. In that silent, desolate place I felt loneliness like I had never felt before. Resigned, I dropped the cleaning bucket, and bottles of cleaner fell over; I jerked to snatch them up lest the carpet be marked with bleach spots, and walked through the kitchen into what I supposed was the bedroom.

I thought about running across the street to the gas station for food, but I had no money, and besides, Mom had locked me in. *If my old babysitter Lynda were here, she would bring me food from the gas station,* I thought, with the hopeless realization that there was no way out. I started to work, singing while I cleaned. I knew many songs by heart, from the hymnal in my home and from going to church all my life, and had already committed countless verses to memory so that I could sing them to the Lord while I cleaned at home. I began with one of my favorite songs, "Precious Lord, Take My Hand," and followed it with another and another, hearing in my mind the harmonies and the instrumental accompaniment as I cleaned and scrubbed. My fingers became raw with the constant friction and the corrosiveness of the cleaners, so that all my fingertips began to bleed. I kept changing hands to give each arm a break.

Well, I'll be very strong after all this, I thought optimistically. *If Ann knew, she would hug me right now.* That was a consoling thought. I didn't have my Bible with me, but that didn't matter; I could think of all the Scriptures I'd memorized, many of them through song. When I was younger, Mom had bought us a set of tapes of kids singing Scripture; it was always easier to memorize something in the form of a song, and I had learned a lot of verses that way. At first

I wasn't sure I would remember all of the words, but as I began to sing, they popped into my mind. *This is why I've spent so much time learning about God and reading the words of Jesus and the apostles,* I thought. *For this very moment! Years of study and prayer are bearing good fruit right now. This is something Mom can never ever take away from me.*

I finished cleaning after the sun went down. It was dark in the apartment. I thought of turning on the light, but I didn't want to draw attention to my presence in the apartment alone. I lay resting on the bare floor and tried to fight off my loneliness with good thoughts. At least I was away from the threat of Mom's slaps, for instance. I thought of the book *A Little Princess*: at least here there were no mice, and no leaky roofs. I was in a clean, dry place which was now free even of spiders and cobwebs.

But it didn't quite work. In spite of my efforts to be positive, I was overcome with the realization that I was to all intents and purposes a slave, that my life had been completely stripped from me, and in my despair I curled up into a tight ball and cried out to God.

"How? How, Lord? How can I forgive my mother for all the cruel things she has done to me?" The next instant I heard the voice of Jesus say, "Estella, I forgave from the cross. I forgave from the cross." I let the words sink in. What was Jesus saying to me? The cross was the moment of his greatest agony and rejection; in that very moment, while we were perpetrating the most hateful crime against him, he had forgiven. I didn't have to try and forgive Mom. All I had to do was let Jesus forgive through me. I repeated to myself over and over again, "Jesus, you forgave from the cross. You forgave from the cross. You forgave from the cross."

Exhausted and emotionally drained, I began to cry as I sang another song:

For the Lord is faithful.
For the Lord is faithful and
He will strengthen and protect you,
from the evil one, from the evil one.

I sang those words, taken from 2 Thessalonians 3:3, over and over. My voice cracked with the sound of my sobbing as I tried to sing at the same time, but the words and the comforting melody brought peace to my heart. I knew Jesus was present with me there, and He was my Peace. I felt tenderness; I felt safe. He was faithful and would protect me. "I believe you are faithful," I prayed aloud, and reflected on the faith Jesus must have had in His own Father while He hung helplessly on the cross. The whole world would have thought it a hopeless moment, but not Jesus. *How did you make it through those hours on the cross, Lord?*

"I saw my Father on the other side, Estella," Jesus answered. "As I saw the cross looming before me, I saw my Father smiling at me from behind it, with His arms around it." I thought about this as I continued singing "For the Lord is Faithful," and soon I dropped off to sleep.

Just as everything else in my life had passed, my lonely time in the empty apartment passed too. Mom picked me up the next day. She furnished the apartment sparsely and used it during the day as a quiet place to get away from the noise of the bulldozers in our area and do school with my brother.

The area we lived in was quickly developing. Mom became very angry that we had acquired neighbors; they were too close, she thought. I couldn't understand why it upset her so much, as I didn't think they were that close, but Mom said she had to get away. The neighbors had raised their property so it would be level with ours and built a two-story house on it, and Mom, in one of her paranoid episodes, said to me that she knew the neighbors were peering from their second-story window into the courtyard. That was where she frequently hit me because of my lack of attention to pruning the rosebushes. Later, when they put the house up for sale, Mom bought it as soon as it went on the market.

One night Mom yelled at Dad, saying she was throwing him out of the house because of me. He was to go to the apartment and take me with him. She did this more and more often as the months went by. During the day she kept me by her side, whether at home or at the apartment, but at night she threw me out of the house to get rid of me. I didn't dare look at Dad on these occasions; I felt sorry that he had to leave because of me. He and I spent many silent nights at the apartment. I could have enjoyed my time with him alone, but Mom had made that impossible; she had succeeded in alienating him from me. How could he love me when I was the source of all his trouble? After a year, Mom decided the apartment was too great an expense. This too had passed.

I was now old enough to get my learner's permit in preparation for getting my driver's licence. Mom sent me to the high school for driving lessons, and I was refreshed by this brief time spent out of the house. I enjoyed being with the other students, and my teacher was very kind. Everyone at school said, "Estella is high on God. She doesn't need drugs." I was very surprised that my joy in Jesus was so obvious, and glad that others could see how much he meant to me.

Soon after this period in my life, God did a miracle in me one night. I was asleep and dreamed I saw the power of God over my town, driving evil far, far away from me. I felt the earth shake beneath my feet and saw a bright cloud filled with a glorious presence. I woke up feeling like I had just been struck by lightning, and at first I couldn't move. Crying tears of joy and overwhelming awe, I finally managed to drag myself out of bed to sit in the other half of the house, where no one could hear me cry. In the game room I sat down on the couch and buried my head between my knees and cried. I couldn't speak. The sense that God was so big and so very powerful flooded my being. After an hour I finally went back to bed, but I was awake for the rest of the night.

The next morning I told Mom and Dad what had happened to me. I explained that God had shown me His almighty power in a dream. I was surprised to find that even though I had slept little, I was fully energized that day. Over the next year, Mom couldn't stop saying how much I had changed. She kept saying that I had changed, and then she began to admit that she had not changed. She would slap me and then cry, and say, "You have changed. You have changed, but I haven't."

On my sixteenth birthday, I was given another dream. This time I heard angels singing, "Fall on your knees in joy and adulation. Fall on your knees in joy and adulation." At the end of this praise to the Lord, an angel said to me, "Make a wish." As soon as I heard those words, I woke up, dropped to my knees, and prayed, "Lord Jesus, I want to see Ann. I haven't seen Ann in a very long time. I want to see Ann for my sixteenth birthday." Then I opened my eyes and stood up. God alone knew what a seemingly impossible request I had just made; Mom rarely went anywhere, let alone with me. I was making my bed when suddenly Mom burst into my room.

"Come on," she said, without wishing me a happy birthday. "Let's go. I need to go to the chiropractor, and you are coming with me." I could hardly contain my excitement. I had to hide my joy, though, or Mom would never let me leave the house again. I calmly stepped into the car and prayed silently that when we arrived at the chiropractor, Ann would be there.

Mom was checked in and placed on the rolling table. Since I wasn't there for an adjustment, I was allowed to go and see Ann. I ran to her office and found her sitting right there at her desk. Calling me by her special nickname for me, Suggums, she swallowed me in a hug and we enjoyed a long, warm, comfortable visit together. That day Mom and Dad forgot my birthday, but God did not. He loved me, and would never forget me. Jesus made it happen. Only God could perform a miracle like this on my birthday!

I didn't know why my parents wanted me to get my driver's licence, since they never let me go anywhere anyway. The days continued to pass monotonously. Day in and day out, Gabriel and I cleaned the house and tried to satisfy our hunger pains by secretly sneaking food. We had discovered that, like the hundred-dollar bills, food in larger quantities could be taken without Mom noticing. Mom ordered food by the case from the Co-Op. We would usually get English muffins, whole wheat sprouty bagels, and whole wheat tortillas, and store them in the fridge or freezer till they were needed.

"Estella, you need to strip the fridge today, because the Co-Op food will arrive soon," said Mom one morning. I trembled at the thought of "stripping" the fridge, as she always put it. She was even more particular about the fridge than the stove, and had the most exacting standards of cleanliness for it. I began gingerly removing the glass shelves, carefully working off the seal that lined the front of each one. Then I scrubbed everything with a toothbrush, running the soft bristles along the soft, flexible seal. That done, I filled a bowl with hot, soapy water, leaned into the fridge, and began cleaning. I craned my neck to see the back of the fridge where the drawers usually hung; I had taken them out to wash by hand. Sometimes, pieces of food fell down from the upper shelves into the bottom of the fridge.

Mom hates crumbs, I thought, my hands growing steadily colder. As I scrubbed everything vigorously with the toothbrush, fresh cuts opened up at my fingertips, stinging the skin under my nails. When I was through scrubbing, I wiped all the surfaces down meticulously and then began shining the freshly washed shelves with Windex, being sure to use as little paper towel as possible. Suddenly my head whipped back as Mom yanked the back of my shirt.

"Estella, you need to clean in the cracks with the terry-cloth rag before you put the shelves back in," Mom said sternly as she slapped me across the face.

"Okay, Mom." I made a mad dash for the laundry room, where I knew I would find more clean rags. I wet one of them in the warm soapy water and set to work finishing my task. After making sure the little knobs on my terrycloth rag made their way successfully into each tiny crack, I buffed everything with another dry, fresh rag. The fridge was now ready for fresh cargo from the Co-Op.

The bagels always came five to a package, and were kept in the large freezer in the laundry room. Gabriel and I knew that if we took just one bagel, Mom would instantly discover it, but if we took an entire package, she would never notice. Our prime opportunity to eat anything was during bath time, because this was the only time either of us was allowed to shut a door. The punishment for locking the door being less severe than the punishment for getting caught with food, I always locked the door when eating anything during bath time.

Mom kept the laundry room freezer locked, but getting hold of the key was no problem for my brother and me.

Then we waited for an opportune time to grab a package of bagels or tortillas, alternating between the two so as not to arouse suspicion; tonight it would be bagels. After successfully obtaining a package of whole wheat sprouted bagels, I ran off to my room and was soon in the bathroom, carefully pushing in the little button on the door to lock it. I started running my bath water, making it as hot as I could possibly stand it, and climbed into the tub; as it began to fill up, I took out two frozen bagels and held them over the hot running water so that just the steam touched them.

I watched the thawing process with hungry joy, waiting patiently for the hot steam to make its effect. Mom bought only very healthy foods; this bagel had whole pieces of grain sticking out of it. I liked the raisin bagels better, but we couldn't always pick what we were going to sneak. By the time the tub was full, the outer layer of each bagel was thawed. Biting down on my first bagel, I firmly scraped off a bite with my teeth and breathed a sigh of satisfaction, rejoicing that Mom was not around to cut my bagel into fourths and give me only one piece. I ate off all of the thawed portion, leaving the center still frozen hard; what could I do with it? I was running out of time. My tub was full and I needed to save hot water for my brother. I dunked the remaining part of the bagel into the hot tub water and wolfed it down. It was now partly soggy and only partly thawed, but I was so hungry I didn't care.

With an uneven number of bagels in each bag, Gabriel and I always shared the last bagel; I had already stowed my half in a board game and would save it for tomorrow. Climbing out of the tub, I watched the water drain as I wrapped a towel around myself, then rinsed the tub thoroughly and inspected the area for evidence. All trace of the bagels was gone.

"It's your turn," I called out to my brother. Going into my closet, I ducked under the clothes so I could see through the vent and watch out for Mom as Gabriel smuggled his share of the bagels into the bathroom. He always watched out for me. Finally, I heard the door to the tub area close. We'd pulled it off again.

29

Night Ride

Mom asked me one day to go with her to an old building.
She had made a sizable donation to an organization, and her
only request was that she be allowed to take from a certain
building whatever she wanted. They were more than happy
to grant her request, and Mom took me along, saying she
needed my help with a new project.

At the site, I stepped out of the car and stared at what
was apparently a deserted old building. Mom turned a key
in the rusty lock and pushed the door open, motioning me
to follow her in. The smell of mildew filled my nostrils,
faintly recalling the moldy cake I had eaten years before,
and I sneezed as I struggled to breathe in the musty
atmosphere.

It was dark, and there was no electricity; only the light
from the windows illuminated the randomly stacked boxes

spotted with cat feces. It was raining outside and water dripped dismally from the ceiling.

"I want you to load all these boxes into the car," said Mom.

"Yes, Ma'am. What's in them?" I lifted the flap of a box and peered inside. In the dim light I made out the shapes of many books.

"I'm not sure. We'll take them all home now and then decide what to keep later." I lifted box upon box into the car and unloaded them at the other end as we made several trips to home and back again. The books were heavy, and the boxes were mushy with damp and mildew; I struggled to keep them in one piece as I carried each one to the car, climbing over trash and old forgotten things on my way to the door. At one point I felt water dripping on me and looked up at the leaky ceiling. How could anyone want anything from a place like this? But all the books finally made their way to our home, filling our garage and kitchen with their musty smell. There were hundreds of them.

"Estella, these books are dirty," said Mom, stating the obvious. "I want you to clean them all. Every page of each and every book."

"We're going to keep them *all*?"

"Oh, yes, we'll keep them all; we must not waste any. We'll line the game room with bookcases and fill them with all our new books."

I sat down to begin my formidable task, using a cloth slightly dampened with bleach. Day after day found me sitting on the cold tile floor in the kitchen, cleaning page after page of each book as the hours stretched on interminably. So many pages to clean! The smell of mildew became my morning greeting, afternoon hello, and goodnight kiss. I played my music when I could, and when I could not,

I sang. At the end of each long day I reveled in my bedtime, falling asleep every night with the same music box under my pillow while it played "A Stranger in Paradise."

One night, however, I was awakened by a crash: while sleeping I had thrust my hand under my pillow, knocking the porcelain music box up against the wall at the head of my bed so that it shattered. I cried as I fingered the broken pieces. I would have to find a way to glue them back together. To comfort myself, I let my thoughts go to our upcoming Co-Op pick up, when I would get to see Ann again. Ann would give me a hug, and then I would feel better.

Mom's collection of old moldy books was not the only manifestation of her obsession with acquiring stuff cheap: she had also begun to frequent garage sales. She couldn't make us go with her all the time, as she was afraid it would arouse suspicion if people saw that we were not in school. So whenever she went alone on her quests, Gabriel and I enjoyed some time on our own in the house. Her return, however, always resulted in a fresh batch of work.

She bought depression glass, but also a lot of worthless old clothes, mounds of which began accumulating in the game room. One day Dad couldn't even get into the house from the garage, because the floor was buried under clothes to such a depth that the door to the garage could not be opened. Mom always had me do all the sorting, washing, ironing, and mending. I was required to sew up little holes by hand, since Mom had not yet taught me how to sew with a machine. She often purchased old torn sheets as well, and stacked them up in the game room closet.

"I've bought these old sheets so that I can teach you how to sew," Mom informed me one day. I stared in horror at the seven-foot stacks of sheets that filled the closet from floor to ceiling, evoking once again the fairy tale of Rumpelstiltskin.

It will take me the rest of my life to sew all this, even with a machine! Please, God, no! Please, God, no! I prayed fervently. Mom cleared a small space for me to sit down in front of the sewing machine and was starting to show me how to use it, when suddenly she was distracted. Since I was obliged to stay close to her side at all times, I followed her dutifully into the other room, where she soon forgot about the stacks of old sheets in the closet. I was left with Dad's and Gabriel's old socks to mend instead, which I could do while watching whatever Mom had on the television at the time. I had escaped the sheet project for now, but it still loomed in the distance.

Every week Gabriel and I found ways to eat the food we so desperately wanted and needed. There were no opportunities to eat away from home, because I was only let out of the house to attend services at our new church, and sometimes a worship committee meeting, where I was involved in the music side of things. Long before we had changed churches, Mom had quit going with us, but now she always came along, keeping a watchful eye on me. The only time I escaped her gaze was during Sunday School, if we went. Sometimes in Sunday School I would sneak a donut, but an uneasy conscience made me ambivalent about doing this very often, torn as I was between obeying my parents and filling my stomach. Mom continued to remark that I had changed for the better, and the dissonance between her observation and the deception I was practicing seemed particularly pointed to me when I was in Sunday School.

Mom also continued to maintain that she had *not* changed, and that was certainly accurate. She seemed better some days, giving me hope that she was going to change, but then she would inevitably revert to her old ways of hitting and slapping me. Not only that, but she was beginning to target my brother more too as he grew older. I couldn't believe she had the guts to hit a teenage boy; I was also amazed that Gabriel never fought back. But like me, he was small.

Meanwhile he and I still had to struggle with constant hunger, and sometimes the temptation to sneak food was too great. And now and then, the longing to eat something besides bagels, tortillas, tuna, and vegetables was overwhelming. But how to get hold of it when we couldn't leave the house, and had no money?

"Okay. Let's do it today, while she takes her bath," I said to Gabriel one day.

"But Mom will be so close! Her bathroom is just a few feet from the closet door," protested Gabriel with a shudder.

"I know, but she won't suspect anything if I'm in there reading to her like always. You can do it right under her nose."

"Okay, Estella. I'll do it then."

When the time came I kept Mom company in the bathroom as usual, reading from a textbook at her request.

"The Civil War was an important time in history," I calmly read aloud while Gabriel noiselessly carried out his exploits. Soon Mom excused me, finished with her morning routine of taking a bath and getting dressed. I did not have a chance to confer with Gabriel about the outcome of his stealth mission, but at lunchtime Dad came home, and I heard him and Mom talking in the back of the house through the vent in my closet.

"I know that I had eight twenty-dollar bills in the closet. I *know* I had! And now there are only five. Some are missing," said Mom to Dad. I gasped as I pulled back from the closet vent. *Oh, my gosh.* I could still see Mom's and Dad's feet on the carpet in their bedroom as they slowly headed toward the hallway. Dad left to go back to the office and I ran to have a conference with Gabriel.

"Gabriel, she knows! Mom knows you took money from the closet. We have to put it back, and then you'll have to clear out while I tell her. You can go a little way up the Mountain and wait there till she calms down."

"Okay," he said. So the next morning, while Mom took another bath, Gabriel raced out the back door and disappeared behind our house into the brush. I trembled with fear as I finally went to Mom and told her what Gabriel had done.

"Gabriel took the money from the closet, and he's put it back," I said.

"Where is your brother now?"

"I sent him up on the Mountain, because I didn't want you to hurt him."

"Go and get him," Mom commanded. "I won't hurt him." So I went outside and called to my brother. I expected him to be right behind our fence, just on the edge of our property, but there was no answer, and no sign of him. I called more urgently, but there was still no response. I began to get scared. Where had he gone? I had told him to go up on the Mountain, not far away. I went back into Mom's bedroom.

"He's not out there."

"Then where is he?"

"I don't know. I don't know where he went. He wasn't supposed to go far away," I said, desperately.

"This is all your fault, Estella!" Mom yelled. She began slapping and hitting me.

After hours had passed and there was still no sign of Gabriel, Mom got on the phone and called Dad, who came home from work right away and went out in the car to search the streets. By late afternoon, Dad had located Gabriel at a friend's house in another neighborhood. Gabriel had hiked far away to see his friend, and because he'd gone in the middle of the day, his ears were blistered from the sun; we weren't used to being outside when the sun was at its highest, since Mom only allowed us out after four in the afternoon.

Dad brought Gabriel back into the house. After the agonizing hours of waiting, I was relieved to see my brother again. Mom's reaction was not like mine, though. At the sight of my brother and his beet red ears, she dropped to her knees on the white carpeted floor and screamed.

"My baby! My baby! You hurt my baby, Estella, you hurt my baby!" she shrieked again and again, clasping my brother's poor ears in her hands. Then she excused him from the room and looked over at me, and the look in her eyes terrified me. Suddenly she leapt through the air, landing on top of me with a thud. Dad watched as Mom began to pummel my body; then he walked over and grabbed her, throwing her off me. I didn't care. Mom was right: I had hurt my brother. It had been my idea to take the money. It was all my fault.

We all recovered from that fateful day, but a seed of terror had been planted in my heart. Mom never again looked at me the same way. I remembered how Dad had come to my rescue that day, but it was only one occasion out of many, and he was not close by very often.

Gabriel and I made our second and last desperate attempt to get food by means of another midnight bike ride to Walmart. We were again successful in keeping it secret, hiding the food on the Mountain like before, and Mom never found out. This time was different though; I was changing. It didn't feel good to eat food that my Mom didn't know about, and it certainly didn't feel good to steal her money. I was afraid God would be displeased with me. I couldn't stand the thought.

Nevertheless, I felt a growing cloud of depression and hopelessness creep over me as I faced the fact that Mom would never let me out of the house. She talked about college sometimes, but she always said that if I left her, I would be hurting her and not loving her. She reminded me of what she had told me when I was only nine: "If you ever leave me, I will cut you off without a cent and then you'll come crawling back to me." I couldn't picture myself ever getting out to do anything, let alone leave Mom for good. It was hard to keep despair at bay, but I remembered reading in *Anne of Green Gables* how Marilla had always said, "To despair is to forsake faith in God."

We arrived at church one Sunday morning as usual, and climbed the stairs to the balcony. I smiled and greeted each person that passed me on our way to the seats we usually occupied; Mom always wanted to sit as far away as she could from everyone else. But as I greeted people I suddenly became conscious of having to hide behind my smile, of just how much secret suffering I had to hold under the surface around other people. Just preparing to come to church filled me with pain, because leaving the house once a week reminded me that a world existed outside my home, that there was a normal kind of life from which I was excluded. Other smiling faces reminded me that other people were kind and Mom was not. I sat down in my seat, overwhelmed by the thought of my life continuing as it was.

When the man playing the offertory sat down and struck the first chord on the piano, I was enraptured. He was playing the familiar hymn, "It Is Well with My Soul." The flowing melody and beautiful harmonies enveloped me in calm and comfort, and I felt a fresh strength. I was very familiar with the story behind the song: the author had written it after losing his wife and two daughters at sea, and penned the words as he passed the very spot where they had drowned. I knew all the words by heart, and heard them in my mind as I listened to the strains of that beloved hymn. They were words of peace, courage, hope, and trust in God: another gift from him, who always seemed to know what I needed.

30

Near-Death Experiences: Dad and Me

During the summer as I neared my seventeenth birthday, I was allowed to go to Dallas to visit my grandparents. This was a surprise, since Mom had sworn some time back that I would never again see my relatives after I had become so attached to them. The trip included a church family conference, which I enjoyed, but I was plagued the whole time by thoughts of having to return home, and was increasingly gripped by paralyzing fear. During a prayer time, several leaders had prayed for me. One of them quoted the verse, "Though my father and mother forsake me, the Lord will take me up" (Psalm 27:10). I was only able to cry; I knew I could never tell anyone what my mom was like or why I felt so afraid. But the trip refreshed me, and I wiped away the tears and resolved to return home with renewed hope.

Gabriel and I returned to a nightmare. Mom ratcheted up the physical attacks on both of us, hitting us routinely, and I was increasingly the target of her verbal attacks as well. I hardly saw Dad; I was not allowed to speak with him or Gabriel, and only spoke with my brother when Mom was not around. Every day we cleaned the house and did school. I was now certain I would never get out, that Mom would likely keep me home forever. I could no longer sneak food as often, either, as the price I paid in guilt and fear was not worth it. I resorted to eating uncooked oats by the handful from the forty-pound bags Mom purchased at the Co-Op. I knew beyond doubt that she would never notice missing oats, and they were very filling and easily accessible.

My brother began to mock me. "I don't see any manna coming down from heaven for you," he said again and again, referring to my trust in God to take care of me. I ignored him. I knew that to maintain my own sanity, I had to stop sneaking food. But how would I avoid starving in that case? Little did I know the strange way in which God would feed me. He knew the food I really needed was not something you could put in your mouth, that I was starving for a different food: love. I longed for hugs. I wanted someone to hold me. And I wanted to be free from fear and oppression and constant apprehension.

It was Saturday, and Dad had decided to repair an outlet in the game room. Mom was in the kitchen keeping busy. I was in the kitchen too, working close to the glass table, when I felt a sudden stomachache. I had felt fine one minute before, and was bewildered by the sudden onset of pain. Unnoticed by Mom, I slipped out of the kitchen; maybe she thought I was off to the bathroom. I went into my bedroom and lay down for about thirty minutes, after which I had a strong urge to get up. I walked through the little brown doors into the living room, past the piano, and into the kitchen. It was now empty.

That's strange, I thought, and kept walking into the game room were Dad had been working. I was shocked at what I saw. My dad lay on the floor, and in the center of his chest a pool of fresh blood had stained his white T-shirt. Mom was walking in circles, unable to function or respond.

"Dad!" I yelled. "Are you okay? What happened? Are you okay? What happened to your chest? Dad! Your chest!"

"I got electrocuted," he managed. "It's not my chest, it's my finger." His hand was resting on his chest and he raised it slightly, exposing a severe slash in his finger. I had never seen a wound so deep. I quickly inspected the rest of his body, and everywhere I looked there were dark blood-like spots where the electricity had exited. I stood up and grabbed Mom by the shoulders.

"Mom!" I yelled boldly; yelling was not something I normally dared to do when speaking to Mom. "Mom, you have to take Dad to the hospital, now!" I pressed the keys into her listless hands and she finally began to take action as we helped Dad to his feet. I watched anxiously as they drove away to the hospital. Dad was a competent handyman. What had gone wrong? I asked myself the same question over and over as I awaited their return. When they finally returned, Dad explained.

"I was working on the outlet and had it exposed. I kept turning the electricity on and then off and then on again. Evidently, I got confused: I thought the electricity was off when it was still on. I touched the wires and the current began to flow through my body, until suddenly this slash appeared and I was thrown off the current."

"Were you holding anything sharp in your hand?" I asked.

"No. I have no idea how the deep cut appeared, but the doctors said that it saved my life. They told me that the electric current would have held me until it gave me a heart attack, except the slicing of the tendon in my finger cut the current. I have to have surgery now on the finger."

"Wow," I said.

The appointment was soon scheduled, and since Mom didn't much like leaving the house, I was elected to transport Dad to the hospital for surgery. It would take place in another town about an hour away.

I'm seventeen now. I can do this, I thought. Dad climbed into the car long before the sun had risen, and I drove him to the hospital. As they wheeled him away, I prayed for him: *Dad is so sensitive to anesthesia, like me; please, God, let him be okay.* When the surgery was complete, the surgeon informed me that the tendon in Dad's hand had been perfectly sliced by something obviously razor sharp.

"Was your father holding anything in his hand when he was electrocuted?" he asked.

"No," we both answered.

"Well, whatever cut his tendon saved his life. If it hadn't been so swiftly and perfectly cut, he would be a dead man right now. I and the other surgeons all agree that the tendon appears to have been cut by a very sharp object, such as a surgeon's knife. Very curious indeed."

"It must have been an angel," I said. "Wow, Dad, an angel cut your hand so that you wouldn't die! Wow!" I managed to help Dad into the car, and he threw up all the way home.

Dad was unable to drive for quite some time after his surgery, a circumstance which forced Mom to let me out of the house; I was a better candidate than herself for running all of Dad's office errands around town. I could hardly contain my excitement at this; I felt bad for Dad, but I felt so liberated! Every day took me to the post office to collect the mail, and to other buildings very close to Ann's office to run a variety of errands. Whenever I had a spare moment, I would run in to see her and she would give me a quick hug before sending me on my way.

This made for a very pleasant break in the day; however, it gave rise to a new problem. Being at home had been more bearable when I was locked away for months on end. Now that I was going out every day, each return to my home felt like another step in a long, slow, gruesome death. Mom was uncontrollable and arbitrary. Her hitting and slapping were constant and made it terrifying to be in her presence. As long as I was away from the house I felt relief, but the prospect of returning home every day filled me with dread. Life at home became unbearable and I trembled any time I was near Mom.

As well as getting out to help Dad, I had begun to teach piano to a little girl down the street, and was also allowed to babysit her sometimes. I was surprised Mom let me do this, but the girl was the daughter of old friends of my parents, and I knew that Mom felt obligated to say yes now and then. Perhaps these things were part of the reason she was so horrible to me at home: she resented my newfound liberty.

As usual, I still read aloud to Mom during her bath. This morning I sat leaning up against her bathroom cupboards, just opposite the tub, reading to her. Mom was already in the tub when she suddenly looked up and ordered me to move the little bathroom trash can from one spot to another about five feet away. I quickly got up, moved the trash can to the newly designated spot, and had just returned to my seat against the cabinets when Mom came flying at me without warning from out of the tub. Before I could even register what was happening, she was on top of me, blocking my vision with her hands as she began vigorously striking my face and body. I felt the sting of wet flesh against my neck and face. Then, almost as suddenly as she had attacked, she jumped off, glaring at me.

"Why did you move that trash can?" she yelled. I was too stunned to reply. I knew for a fact that she had just ordered me to move the trash can. It was at this moment that I understood for certain that it was not I who was to blame, that something was horribly wrong with my mother. She was a very ill person who had grown slack in pursuing treatment and taking her meds. I cried and left her presence as quickly as possible.

Now I had to run off to the office; I couldn't be late with Dad's payroll. I got into the car and drove off, and before I knew it the job was done and I was able to take a few minutes to run into Ann's office.

"Hi, darlin'. How are you today?" she asked, swallowing me in a bear hug. I let go and looked up at her. Although the marks Mom had made were probably gone by now, I could not hide the pain that showed through my eyes.

"Things are not good at home. Things are not good at home," I replied.

"What do you mean, Estella?"

"Things are not good at all," I repeated. I couldn't stop holding on to Ann; the thought of going back home was terrifying. I hugged her again, not wanting to let go.

"What do you mean, Estella?" Ann persisted. Then, looking me intently in the eyes: "Is your Mom abusing you?"

"Yes," was all I could say. "Yes." A weight fell off me at that moment, as I finally gave up my secret, but I knew I still had to go home. I felt again the iron grip of fear: I needed to return home before Mom suspected that I was not at the usual places accomplishing work for Dad.

"I have to leave now. May I call you sometime?"

"Yes, Estella. You can call me anytime." I looked back longingly at Ann as I disappeared through the back office door. I stepped into Dad's car and drove off to the office to drop off the mail.

I was home before lunch; Dad had not suspected a thing. Removing my shoes in the garage, I walked into the house, but as soon as I crossed the threshold I was again overcome by a tsunami of fear. I shook as I made my way through the game room, down the hallway and into the kitchen. Mom was dressed and standing by the kitchen sink.

"Estella, wipe off the cabinet over there," she said, pointing to the other side of the kitchen. I began wiping off the cabinet as I looked out the little window over the counter. I could see past the trees to my town in the distance, and longed to be outside again. Moving all the canisters that lined the countertop, I carefully wiped behind them as Mom popped a potato into the microwave for lunch; she was standing right next to me as she waited for the potato to cook, as she had always believed it was unwise to stand directly in front of the microwave while it was running. *My, how things have changed*, I thought as I remembered watching crayon shavings melt a decade before, *and yet how little.* Mom moved closer to me and suddenly raised both hands. I flinched, but she didn't strike me this time.

"I'm trying not to pulverize your body," she screamed frantically, wrapping both hands loosely around my neck. "I'm trying not to kill you. I'm trying not to kill you, you arrogant little bitch. You and O.J. are one and the same!" Mom's arms shook as she stretched them out; her hands were still loose around my neck, but she was shaking with the effort of resisting the impulse to strangle me. She pulled her hands away, and then brought them back again, cupping them around my neck so that her thumbs were almost touching in front of my throat. I stood there, motionless; after seventeen years of just taking it from Mom, the thought of moving backwards didn't even occur to me. Mystified over what could possibly have triggered this behaviour, and petrified into paralysis, I stood staring into Mom's eyes.

"I'm trying not to kill you," Mom repeated. I believed her. The vein on the front of her forehead was bulging and her entire face was red with fury. I was still trying to puzzle out why Mom was so angry with me, as she had given no explanation. Had I missed a spot on the counter, or misplaced a canister? The beeper went off on the microwave, and as Mom backed up and withdrew the potato, I silently returned to my job of wiping off the kitchen counters. Mom seemed to calm down as she ate her potato. I felt like I had narrowly avoided death; I was so scared, I didn't care that I wasn't getting anything to eat.

"Estella," Mom said one day after another of her endless garage sale circuits, "I want you to wash all the new glasses I picked up today." I turned and looked across the room at the counter completely covered by rows of plain, clear drinking glasses. We already had a host of dishes. I opened the cabinet above the kitchen sink, then the ones next to them on either side, surveying their crowded contents and trying to figure out where on earth I would put the new glasses. I began carefully loading each glass into the dishwasher and watched as Mom went over to the blender and took out a container of nonfat powdered milk. Her back toward me, she dropped a single scoop of the powder into the blender and then walked with it over to the sink where I was working.

"Here, I need four cups of water in this blender." According to the directions on the package, it was one cup of water per scoop of powdered milk, but Mom liked to make everything go as far as possible. She thrust the blender into my wet, soapy hands and I grasped the handle firmly, knowing that my quota of watery milk for the day was coming up. I wiped off the blender after filling it and walked it back over to Mom, who seated it on its base and hit the power button. The resulting mixture was not so much white as cloudy. Then she opened a drawer, withdrew one of many detergent bottle lids she had accumulated for measuring portions of food and drink, and poured in the lukewarm mixture to the bottom fill line. Mom didn't allow us ever to use real dishes; I was only allowed to eat off of small plastic Tupperware lids and drink out of the Cheer detergent lids.

"Here is your milk," she said, handing it to me. I drank it down quickly. It didn't taste like the milk I remembered drinking in my early childhood; it was more like water with chalky overtones, water you might get out of a creek bed with clay soil. Plain, clear water would have tasted much better.

I knew I was never to waste a drop. After downing the diluted milk, I filled the detergent lid cup with clean water, swished it around, and gulped it down before putting the lid into the dishwasher with the rest of the dishes. Mom grabbed my arm and sank her fingernails into my flesh as she slapped me across the face.

"Keep the cup for the rest of the day! You know that you are to dirty only one cup a day," she reminded me. I placed the lid on the counter near the spot where I sometimes, but rarely, sat down to eat, and went back to loading the dishwasher with the garage sale glasses, my hands shaking.

"I'm trying not to pulverize your body," Mom said again; it was becoming her mantra. "Now I want you to wash all the depression glass by hand."

I breathed a sigh of relief: all the black depression glass was in another room, so fetching it gave me the opportunity to leave Mom's presence, even if only for a moment. I made several trips, carefully carrying dish after dish into the kitchen, and spent the rest of the afternoon and late into the evening handwashing and drying each piece. The depression glass wasn't actually dirty, but Mom didn't like it to collect a single mote of dust.

That night I lay in bed with eyes wide open, too petrified to sleep, convinced that unthinkable evil must have settled into my home. Only evil would want to kill me. I was afraid Mom might come into my room at night and rip me out of bed to clean, or worse yet, go through with strangling me for real. I couldn't risk falling asleep, but my terror took care of that; I couldn't relax enough to sleep.

The next day I walked into the kitchen dressed and ready to clean, but I felt like a zombie on energy drinks. My heart raced as I began to prepare the hot cereal close to where Mom stood. I needed a wooden spoon to stir it with, which once again posed a dilemma: I did not want to have to ask Mom to step away from the drawer, but letting the cereal burn would be equally likely to arouse her anger. Finally,

Mom stepped a little to the right and I quickly grabbed the drawer. Mom reached over and grasped my wrist.

"I've told you not to open the drawers by the side. I don't want you ever to touch the wood, or you'll ruin it with the oils on your hands. Only grasp the handle," she barked, punctuating her orders with several slaps. "You and O.J. are one and the same. I'm trying not to kill you." Mom's hands stretched out toward my neck again.

"Okay, Mom," I answered quietly, and with forced calm. I stirred the cereal with my left hand as I carefully shut the drawer with my right. After turning the burner to low heat, I raced out of the kitchen on my daily rotation from one corner of the house to the next, adjusting the mini-blinds; I was glad to have yet another excuse to be free of Mom's outstretched arms.

After the usual grind of chores and being scolded and slapped for minute or imagined infractions, it was time for me to leave for Dad's office. Every day I was grateful for this chance to leave the house, and thought about how God had turned a tragedy—Dad's electrical accident—into my salvation. I made visiting Ann a regular occurrence on these trips. I couldn't afford to visit for more than a few minutes, but it was wonderful.

There was one problem, however: these brief daily escapes had given me a taste of freedom from home. The wonder of being away from my torturous environment, and the comfort of being near Ann, who not only loved me but showed it by the way she spoke to me and hugged me, made going back all the more painful. My ability to bear the pain, fear, and constant anxiety at home was beginning to wane. Things had now reached the point where I literally feared for my life every day; but I kept this to myself.

31

Deliverance

After the day I confided in Ann, I was able to see her quite frequently without anyone's knowledge. Ann knew that my life would be in serious danger if Mom ever discovered I had told anyone about the abuse, so she guarded my confidence with the utmost discretion while attempting to determine what to do.

Soon after this, Mom hurt me again on my way out the door to teach piano and babysit. I went to the Hamiltons' house just down the street to work. These were old friends of my parents; Mom and Dad didn't really have relationships with anybody anymore, but they allowed me to babysit the Hamiltons' daughter. After putting the little girl to bed, I contemplated making a phone call to my aunt in Dallas. I would tell her that I wanted to come to Dallas, and would implore her to invent an excuse to have me come and help her out by caring for my cousins. I would say nothing of Mom's abuse. My hope was just that Mom would let me go for a little while at least—on the pretext of helping, of course. And perhaps while there at my aunt's place I could say something to her. But I didn't make the phone call; I couldn't bring myself to take such a risk. If Mom suspected anything, she would kill me—or worse, let me live with her wrath.

"I don't care what you have to do, God, just get me to Dallas," I prayed; I knew that calling God would be much safer than calling my aunt. Then I ate some fresh cake from the cake plate in the Hamiltons' kitchen. I lifted the glass and cut myself a piece, and then went over to the CD player, put in the CD I'd brought, and turned on the music. I sat and listened to my new favorite song many times back to back: "In the Arms of Love," by Michael Bolton. I loved the lyrics; they made me feel that God was lifting me up with his tender and powerful arm. I felt strengthened by the food I had eaten, too.

The Hamiltons finally returned home. Since I did my babysitting at night, I had driven Dad's car, even though home was within walking distance. These days I was constantly exhausted from lack of sleep due to fear; at home, that fear had begun to manifest in nightmares on the few occasions I allowed sleep to overtake me. I plopped exhausted into Dad's vehicle, slowly backed out of the Hamiltons' driveway, and drove down the street towards home.

"Oh no!" I groaned, before I had quite made it home. In my nervous anxiety at having to return home, I had left Mom's CD behind. "She'll skin me alive if she finds out that I took her CD," I said out loud. I turned the car around, not noticing that I was too close to a parked vehicle, and heard a crash as I struck it. I knew I had to go in immediately to Mom and Dad and tell them. Surprisingly, they directed me to go to the neighbors' house and make a confession. I nervously knocked on the door and explained what had happened, and they informed their guest, whose vehicle it was. After we had exchanged insurance information, I was sent home, relieved that no one had seemed too upset—not even my parents. But I knew Mom was unlikely to let the matter rest. It would cause even more tension between the two of us.

The next day I was sent to the Hamiltons' again to teach piano. When the lesson was over, as I turned to leave, the mother of the child approached me.

"Is your Mom abusing you?" she asked quietly.

"Yes," I replied. "Ann knows too." Again I had admitted to it.

I continued on home. I had said nothing to Mrs. Hamilton of just what it was that my mom was doing to me; but I had explicitly confirmed that she was abusing me, and I had mentioned that Ann also knew about it. Mr. Hamilton was an attorney. I could only imagine what might happen next, and felt my nerves beginning to crumble. I still had to return home.

The next day during Mom's shower, I called Ann while Gabriel stood watch at the little brown doors. As long as the shower water was running, Mom could not hear, and we would be safe.

"Estella, I've set up a meeting for tomorrow with the attorney, his wife, and a child abuse counselor. We'll all meet with you and determine together what should be done," Ann assured me.

"I'll be there. Don't worry," I said, and quickly hung up.

I whispered tomorrow's plans to Gabriel, and then we retired to our rooms. After Mom got out of the shower, and having observed that she was in a suitably accommodating frame of mind, I made my move.

"Mom, tomorrow the church would like me to attend a worship committee meeting. May I go?" I asked, without betraying my feelings.

"Yes, you may go," Mom answered. I could hardly believe my ears.

That day I spent every spare moment reading my devotional. I had six different devotional books on my desk. One of them mentioned the day Pearl Harbor was bombed, and I thought, *My life has been bombed.* I felt the weight and terror of the bombing in my own heart. On that horrible day in Pearl Harbor, people had lost loved ones and the nation had reeled in shock. I felt shocked, too, by the inescapable feeling that I would lose my own life: Mom was going to kill me if something didn't happen very soon.

The next day Dad had to work out of town and would not return till late in the evening. He had taken the Suburban and left me the damaged car to drive to my meeting. I was on my way out the door when Mom stopped me. For a moment my heart jumped into my mouth. Had she changed her mind about letting me go?

"Here, take your brother with you," she said. "I want him to go to the library while you're at your meeting."

"Okay, Mom." I silently breathed a sigh of relief. I wasn't sure what the outcome of the meeting would be, but it was just a meeting, so I was sure I'd have no problem bringing my brother back home. After dropping him off, I walked inside the church and through the large double doors into a meeting room, where I sat down with the adults and answered numerous questions. I only realized how long we'd been talking together when Gabriel walked in; he'd returned from the library because it had closed.

To my surprise, he addressed the meeting.

"I'm not worried about myself, but I'm afraid that my mom is going to kill my sister," he declared. I was shocked; I hadn't realized that he was afraid for me. He reached into his pocket and pulled out a small sticky note covered with writing.

"This is the stuff that my mom said to my sister just today," Gabriel said. Someone read the sticky note aloud:

I'm trying not to kill you.

I'm trying not to pulverize your body.

You arrogant little bitch. You and O.J. Simpson are one and the same.

I was stunned at my brother's initiative. I had no idea he had even noticed what Mom had been saying to me. I myself hadn't even registered all that she had said to me that day.

"Yeah, Mom says this stuff to Estella all the time. I'm afraid she is really going to kill her," Gabriel continued.

"Well," said the attorney, "you're not going home tonight. Neither of you is going home tonight. What you both have been experiencing is truly abuse, and you are not going home tonight." He repeated it to make sure it sank in.

"We're not?" I asked in disbelief. It was beyond what I had hoped. I didn't have to go home! I didn't have to go back to that place of fear and dread.

"No. You are not," came the firm reply. The attorney rose to his feet and left the room. After several phone calls to relatives in Dallas, it was decided that Gabriel and I would be sent to live with my aunt and grandparents. It was now dark outside, and I became worried, knowing that Dad and Mom must surely be wondering where we were.

"We should have arrived safely back home a long time ago," I commented anxiously.

"Don't worry, Estella, the attorney will call your dad and tell him where you are," Ann assured me. After some discussion, it was decided that we would all go together to my other grandparents' house, Dad's parents. I had not seen them in a very long time, as Mom had forbidden it.

Before long Gabriel and I were standing on their porch together with the attorney, Ann, and the counselor. My grandparents were surprised to see so many people at such a late hour and welcomed us in. A moment later Gabriel and I were escorted to the back of the house as my Dad arrived and was intercepted by Ann.

"You do not say those things to a child," I heard Ann tell Dad with crisp authority. I smiled. I had never seen anyone stand up for me that way. Gabriel and I went into the bedroom, not wanting to hear what else would be said to Dad. I didn't even want to see Dad at all. I was scared.

"Estella, your father wants to see you," someone said to me. I emerged trembling from the bedroom and faced my father.

"Please come home," Dad coaxed. "Your mother is sorry for hitting you. Please come home, Estella. She won't hit you." But I was not persuaded. I gathered my courage and looked my father in the eye.

"No, Dad. I won't go home." I knew my mother too well. Mom had often said she was sorry and promised to stop hitting me—sometimes even as she was in the very act! Now that she knew I'd told someone, she would kill me for sure if I went back home. "Mom can't help but hit me, Dad," I said. "She can't control it."

"The children are going to stay with family members in Dallas. They are not to see their mother, but they do need to go home to collect some of their things. See to it that their mother is not there when they come," ordered the attorney.

I was still having difficulty believing that this was happening. After Dad left, Gabriel and I came out of the back bedroom. Aunt Jean came over, Dad's sister, whom I had not been allowed to see in a very long time; the first thing she asked me was what I wanted to eat.

"I will go get you anything you want: Sonic, Taco Villa, McDonald's, whatever you want. Let's feed you!" urged my aunt with a note of celebratory excitement in her voice. I was overwhelmed. I had never been allowed to eat at any of those places.

"I'd like Taco Villa," I replied. Gabriel made his choice known, and we awaited the arrival of our food. The emotional upheaval had made me a bit sick to my stomach, but I did manage to eat a little. Ann kept hugging me and then finally said she needed to go home.

She came back the next morning. While Ann and my Aunt Jean were there, Dad called to talk to me and then put Mom on the phone.

"I'm sorry for hitting you, Estella. I won't hit you anymore," Mom said in her most convincing penitential tone. Ann and Aunt Jean stood there shaking their heads and vigorously waving their arms as I listened to my mother's pleas.

"No, Mom," I finally said, hesitantly.

"Please, Estella. I won't hit you."

"No, Mom," I repeated, more firmly this time.

Soon Dad was back at my grandparents' house, begging me to come home. Again I looked him in the eye and refused. He confessed that he had done wrong in just going to work every day, turning a deaf ear and a blind eye to everything happening at home; but no amount of apparent remorse was going to change my mind now. Later in the day my aunt and grandmother from Dallas arrived, having left early in the morning to pick my brother and me up. We all stood in a circle and prayed together before we left town. As we prayed I truly felt God filling my heart with peace.

I had recovered my old journal, a few clothes, and some piano music from home. Ann had managed to get my piano music library collection out of the house for me, an expensive set purchased by Mom years before. My Aunt Jean gave me my very own Tony Baxton CD, which I promptly stuck into the new portable player given to me by Granny and Grampy; I clicked the Repeat button and listened to "Unbreak My Heart" all the way to Dallas without saying a word, sad that I had to leave Ann, the only real mother I had ever known. I had been without proper sleep for two weeks and was too tired to speak on the long car ride, but I prayed silently to God every moment to "unbreak my heart" for having to say goodbye to Ann. My only comfort was in knowing that I would never have to say goodbye to God, and that my new home with my aunt and grandparents would be without fear.

ACKNOWLEDGMENTS

To God, the everlasting love of my life. In face-to-face relationship shared among the Father, the Son, and the Holy Spirit I have become what I am. The joy of my salvation is in knowing that we are all included in that beautiful relationship. I have come to understand that even during intense feelings of aloneness and suffering, there is no separation from God, who is love. I have been learning to rest, relax, enjoy life, and above all to love others as I come to know God more each day. My life is a testimony to God's grace and parenting.

To my aunts and uncles, who never gave up loving me and who have adopted me as their own child in every way, to these adopted parents of mine: you have shown me what the true love of God is in daily living. To my maternal grandfather and grandmother, who gave me the first sweet taste of love and the grace of God and revealed to me the "Grace Walk": I will forever thank you and love you for your greatest gift. To my Granny and Grampy who always called me their daughter, I miss you still and look forward to reuniting with you in Heaven.

To all my family and friends who have carried me to the place I am now: this book was only produced by your loving support, help, and constant giving in many ways. This autobiography would not be a reality today without the wisdom and expertise of Debbie, editor; Luke, publisher; Hailee, photographer; Jeff, screen editor; and Emily, model. Thank you all for giving time to the completion of this book with no expectation of material return. May God richly bless y'all, as we say in Texas.

Finally, I cannot fail to thank the great men of faith who have impacted and shaped my life for the last six years: Dr. Baxter Kruger, Dr. Steve McVey, Dr. Brad Jersak, and William P. Young. It has been a pleasure getting to know, learn from, and share faith with you. Thank you for reinforcing the truth about the Trinity and the loving character of God, and for bringing clarity, freshness, and truth to the gospel message. You continue to shape my life through your encouragement, your writing, and many conferences around the world.

"There is a friend who sticks closer than a brother" (Proverbs 18:24). I wish to acknowledge the following friends: Julie, John, Darby, Mike, DJ, Madison, the Phillips family (Kim, Jeff, and Hailee), Lauren, Elizabeth, Suzi, Abby, Christine, LeeDonna, Jill, Bob, Susan, Rebekah, Steven, Claire, Holly, Makenna, Sarah P., Sarah R., Beverly H., Ann and John Michaels, Dawn, Steve, Beckie, Ruth Ann, Deb, and Jamey Caye. Thank you for the incredible encouragement each one of you has brought to me. I could not have survived the last troubling years without you!

To my dearest Rachel: you will always be my sister and the pillar of strength who has stood beside me in every circumstance. Thank you for your never-ending support and sisterly love. My life is enriched by your constant presence and our daily talks. I can always count on you to listen, support, and advise. You will forever hold a special place in my heart as my sister from another mother.